SAINT AUGUSTINE'S

Childhood

GARRY WILLS

SAINT AUGUSTINE'S
Childhood

✤

Confessiones Book One

VIKING

VIKING

Published by the Penguin Group
Penguin Putnam Inc., 375 Hudson Street,
New York, New York 10014, U.S.A.
Penguin Books Ltd, 27 Wrights Lane,
London W8 5TZ, England
Penguin Books Australia Ltd, Ringwood,
Victoria, Australia
Penguin Books Canada Ltd, 10 Alcorn Avenue,
Toronto, Ontario, Canada M4V 3B2
Penguin Books (N.Z.) Ltd, 182–190 Wairau Road,
Auckland 10, New Zealand

Penguin Books Ltd, Registered Offices:
Harmondsworth, Middlesex, England

First published in 2001 by Viking Penguin,
a member of Penguin Putnam Inc.

10 9 8 7 6 5 4 3 2 1

LIBRARY OF CONGRESS CATALOGING-IN-PUBLICATION DATA
Augustine, Saint, Bishop of Hippo.
    [Confessiones. Liber 1. English]
    Saint Augustine's childhood : Confessiones: Book One / [commentary by]
Garry Wills.
        p. cm.
    ISBN 0-670-03001-5 (alk. paper)
    1. Augustine, Saint, Bishop of Hippo—Childhood and youth.   2. Christian
saints—Algeria—Hippo (Extinct city)—Biography.   I. Wills, Garry, 1934–
II. Title.
BR65.A6 E5 2001c
270.2'092—dc21
[B]   2001017987

This book is printed on acid-free paper.

Printed in the United States of America
Set in Aldus with Phaistos display and MT Arabesque Ornaments
Designed by Carla Bolte

TO MY OWN GODSENDS

John, Garry, Lydia

CONTENTS

Key to Brief Citations

Boldface numerals in square brackets [1] refer to paragraphs in Book One of *The Testimony*.

comm. refers to the Commentary on Book One.

O, with volume and page (O 2.52–56), refers to James J. O'Donnell, *Augustine, "Confessions"* (Oxford, 1992).

T, with book and paragraph number (T 10.5), refers to books of *The Testimony* other than Book One.

I translate all Scripture texts from the Latin versions Augustine used. The Psalms are numbered as in the Vulgate bible and in the Douay-Rheims Catholic translation of them.

FOREWORD

It may seem odd to devote a whole volume to one short chapter ("Book") in a not very long work, Augustine's *Confessiones*—though it will not surprise classicists, who are used to separate texts (with commentary) of the various "books" of Homer's epics, or of Virgil's *Aeneid*. I, at least, am not likely to feel uncomfortable with this format, since I wrote a book of over 272 pages on a speech of only 272 words, the Gettysburg Address. And there are reasons to think readers may need more sympathetic exposition of Augustine than of Lincoln, who is closer to us in both geography and time. The American president's world cannot possibly look as exotic as Augustine's African environment and late-antique thought patterns. Besides, the first book of the *Confessiones* (which, for reasons later given, I shall be translating as *The Testimony*) offers special challenges to line-by-line attention. It is a famous source of later controversy in philosophy and theology. It is also, in ways the reader first encountering it may not expect, a source of information for one of the most important relationships in Augustine's life. The book is largely about his son.

Book One covers the first two of the six ages of man into which Augustine divided every human life that ran its full span. Of the first stage, infancy, he remembers nothing, while the most important aspect of the second stage, learning to talk, he remembers accomplishing, though he says that only later did he find out how he had done it. That would seem to give him little to work with in a book covering one period that he does not remember and another period that he did not understand. For both ages, he says, he relies not on direct autobiographical reminiscence but on close observation of other infants: "I have learned that babies act this way, from the ones I had occasion to observe, who, without having known me [as an infant], taught me more about myself than the nurses who did know me"[8]. The most obvious and immediate object of such scrutiny—a scrutiny he kept up at close quarters over a long period of time—was the son he found himself unwillingly saddled with when he was a graduate student. He would soon come to love and even admire this talented youth, who was fated to die when he was seventeen, his father's age at his birth. Called Godsend (*A-Deo-Datus*), the boy elicited this proud statement while he was still alive: "His talent, if a father's fondness deceives me not, is full of promise" (*Happiness in This Life* 1.6). Recalling the time when father and son were baptized together (Godsend was fifteen, Augustine thirty-three), the Bishop of Hippo wrote:

> We made the boy Godsend one of our company [as catechumens], a product of my sinful flesh but of your beneficent creation. He was only fifteen, but in talent he was forging ahead of many older scholars. I testify to your great gifts in him, my Lord God, the creator of everything, able to shape a form out of our deformities—for I had no part in him but my sin, and the

very fact that we had nursed him on your teachings was at your prompting, none other's—it is to your gifts, then, that I bear testimony. In that book of mine called *The Teacher*, he converses with me. You are my witness that all the ideas attributed to my partner in that dialogue were actually his, though he was only sixteen at the time. I had many other experiences of his preternatural ability—it was such that it stunned me, and who could have wrought such marvels but you? Shortly after, you ended his life on earth, but I look back on his life with assurance, with no misgivings about his boyhood or youth—or, if it had come to that, his maturity (T 9.14).

The words "we had nursed him on your teachings" show that Augustine, like his own father, left the boy's religious training to his Catholic mother. This was a providential arrangement, he states, since the boy came to baptism as the culmination of long Catholic training. Augustine had experienced the first stages of such training, but broke it off in his own adolescence.

The dialogue with Godsend, *The Teacher*, was taken down by scribes a decade or so before Augustine wrote the first book of *The Testimony*. That he had the dialogue in mind, and his son's brilliant learning of language, is apparent from the way he returns to the earlier work's themes and very terms when describing how children learn language (see, for instance, [13]). The importance of the dialogue for a correct interpretation of Book One of *The Testimony* can be seen from the most famous attack on Book One. Ludwig Wittgenstein, in the prominent opening passage of his *Philosophical Investigations*, convicts Augustine of a simplistic view of language. But later scholars have demonstrated that Wittgenstein did not understand Augustine's position, which was spelled out more fully in *The Teacher*, and then referred to only briefly in *The Testimony*. Wittgenstein, despite his obvious interest in Augustine's theory of language, seems never to have read the principal source for it, *The Teacher*.

Some scholars have come to realize that Augustine's approach has important similarities to the linguistic school founded by Noam Chomsky, and to laboratory work still being done with children in the various stages of language acquisition. Augustine's startling contention is that no one taught him language. That is the position Chomsky takes—in, for instance, *The Architecture of Language* (Oxford University Press, 2000), page 6:

> [Language acquisition] is also called "learning," but that is a pretty misleading term because it seems more like growth processes than anything that is properly called "learning." You put a child in a situation where the right stimulation is around and acquisition of language is something that happens to the child.

So important is *The Teacher* to a correct reading of Book One (see *comm.* **[13]**) that I print a new translation of the dialogue in an appendix. My frequent references to the dialogue can thus be consulted in their original context, and those interested in the relation of Augustine to his son will have access to its best expression.

ACKNOWLEDGMENTS

I am grateful to Peter Brown and James O'Donnell for their valuable correspondence on Augustinian issues. Also to my editor, Carolyn Carlson, and her assistant, Lucia Watson. My agent, Andrew Wylie, and his assistant, Zoe Pagnamenta, are ever watchful.

PART I

Introduction

1. The Man and His Book

Augustine was born in the era of Late Antiquity, that now much-studied period when the Roman empire was widespread, officially Christian, and not fully aware of the end that was looming for it. Born (354) in an obscure corner of this imperial structure—in the North African town of Thagaste (now part of Algeria)—Augustine, like his parents, thought that the empire offered him a vast staircase he could climb by rhetorical skill (the general coin of achievement and influence) backed by well-cultivated patronage. His father Patrick was a modest landholder and minor Roman official; his mother Monnica was probably from Berber stock and may have been illiterate, though she had a natural shrewdness to match her Christian piety. Their son was sent off, from age twelve to sixteen, to live in a neighboring town (Madauros) for his early literary training. When he returned to Thagaste, his father could not afford to give him the crucial equivalent of graduate school in rhetoric. But Romanian, a Thagaste millionaire with wide connections in the empire, made Augustine his protégé, and after a year of mild hell-raising in Thagaste, Augustine went on to complete his studies in Carthage. He probably took with him a young woman he fell in love with in Thagaste, a woman he would live with for the next fifteen years—"and with her alone, since I kept faith with her bed" (T 4.2). This stable relationship is far from the picture of a sexually promiscuous youth presented by those who have not read Augustine carefully.

Soon after his arrival in Carthage, Augustine's partner bore their first and only child. Augustine admits that the baby was born because he did not take contraceptive measures—which he obviously observed for the rest of his years with the boy's mother. Friends in the Manichaean sect, a fashionable though forbidden religion in the Christian empire, helped Augustine find patronage in Rome, which he reached in 383, at the age of twenty-nine. Within a year, his brilliance was rewarded with appointment as court orator to the young emperor Valentinian II in his western capital of Milan. While in Milan, Augustine met another influential group of thinkers, this time Christian Neoplatonists, and he was soon converted to their philosophical and ascetic tenets. The ideals of this group made him give up his plan to marry into wealth and position, a step he had prepared for by separating himself from his son's mother. But the ties of the flesh were still too great for him to throw them off entirely, and he took a second mistress for a short time. He was unable to break away from her until he had undergone a series of conversion attempts. These reached their crisis in a garden, where he heard an accidental chant that broke down his resistance to grace. He, his son, and some of the protégés he had acquired were baptized on Easter Day, 387, by Ambrose, the charismatic bishop of Milan.

Returned to his African home of Thagaste, Augustine and

his friends planned to found a philosophical monastery for Christian intellectual-ascetics, where Augustine would write an encyclopedic series of works defining Christian humanism. His son was initially part of this community, though he died soon after its formation. Since Augustine was still known in Africa for his earlier defenses of Manichaeism, he wrote some pamphlets denouncing that doctrine. This conflict with Manichaeans laid the basis for a new kind of fame. That fame led Catholics in the harbor town of Hippo, where he chanced to be staying, to demand that he accept ordination as their priest. Since this was the normal way to recruit clergy at the time, and Christians were not normally allowed to hold themselves exempt from such a call, Augustine reluctantly gave up his preferred life of study and prayer and writing, to become a priest at age thirty-seven and a bishop four years later.

He would spend almost forty years, from age thirty-seven to his death at seventy-six, ministering to his small flock at Hippo. He never again left Africa, though he engaged in theological controversy with figures throughout the empire. He addressed topical issues in his flood of letters, sermons, and pamphlets. Early in his tenure as bishop he tried to escape the demanding routine of such occasional writings. This led him, as the fourth century was ending, to undertake three major works not tied to specific controversies—*The Testimony* (begun in 397), *The Trinity* (begun in 400), and *First Meanings in Genesis* (begun in 401). Finishing and polishing these works was his great project of the new century. They introduced "psychological" readings into the mysteries of the Creation and the Trinity.

Only the monumental *City of God*, completed in Augustine's last decades, can compete with the spiritual depths explored in the three central masterpieces of his life, of which *The Testimony* was the inaugural work.

2. *The Book's Genre*

The Testimony is commonly called an autobiography, even "the first autobiography." But that raises expectations, or imposes restrictions, the work cannot support. Autobiography professes to satisfy the expected audience's curiosity about a person's life. But over and over Augustine fails to supply even basic information about himself, or about the events and people that shaped him. We learn that his mother died (though how and of what we are not told), that his son died (though not exactly when or how, or who was present at his death—including, very likely, his mother). His sister is not mentioned, though we know he was close to her, since she superintended a convent annexed to his monastery. He mentions his brother, though not that brother's son, who became a member of his monastery. The family's property dealings are left out. We learn nothing of the officials he dealt with at Valentinian's court, or of the Christian community he came to know in Rome as a recent convert. The man who most influenced his crucial conversion to Neoplatonism, Mallius Theodore, is not even named in *The Testimony*. From his close and intimate circle of Manichaean friends in Carthage, not a single name is recorded. The list could go on.

As surprising as the omissions are the things Augustine includes. Half of Book Two is given over to a youthful theft of pears. Much of Book Three is spent on the death of a nameless friend, while the loss of his beloved son is referred to in just a sentence. There are long disquisitions on time and memory, and—most surprising for those who consider this an autobiography—the last three books do not even mention events in Augustine's life, but comment on the opening of Genesis and on the mystery of the Trinity. If we are to assume that the work has some principle of unity, it is clearly not an autobiographical principle. The work leaves too many things out, and brings too many things in, that offend against that principle.

It may be objected that other famous autobiographies include or exclude much of the subject's life. Henry Adams, in *The Education of Henry Adams*, does not mention his wife or her tragic death. John Henry Newman, in his *Apologia pro vita sua*, does not mention important relations with his brother or his sister. In fact these, along with Rousseau's *Confessions*, are often compared with *The Testimony* as "thesis" biographies— works that use the author's life to argue a certain point of view. Adams uses his baffled attempts at education to argue that the historiography of the United States is in practice unknowable, and he ends with a discussion of potential laws in history. Rousseau argues that his life exemplifies innocence partially corrupted by society, in answer to a "conspiracy" of those accusing him of monstrous behavior. Newman argues that his religious positions were developed consistently, against those accusing him of holding a series of dishonest views. The intended audience, in each case, is made up of those interested in such charges and countercharges. That audience cannot rightly complain if things irrelevant to the book's purpose are omitted or downplayed.

In all three cases, the audience is clearly indicated. Rousseau addresses those who have entertained the attacks on him by *philosophes* as important as David Hume. Newman tells us that he addresses the charges of Charles Kingsley, answering anyone who believes in those charges. Adams admits that his book, privately printed under no author's name, is for a narrow circle of Americans capable of entertaining his dark views. None of these men addresses humankind in general. They have specific people in mind, and they speak directly to them. Augustine, by contrast, does not address any human person. He has an audience of one—God. The entire book is a prayer to him—a point he keeps before his (and our) mind by frequent apostrophe to "Lord" or "God" or "Lord God" or "God my Lord." His language often has the form of liturgical incantation, and the narrative is arranged according to his theological concepts. When he reflects on the fact that his prayer is being taken down by scribes (T 10.3–6), it is only to remark that all men's testimony to God (by word or act) is observable by others, for their own edification, disgust, or self-examination. In *The Teacher* 2, he notes that those who recite psalms in church are praying to God, though they are also reminding each other of God's role in their life. "My heart's fellow will love in me what you, Lord, tell us is lovable, deplore in me what you tell us is deplorable" (T 10.5).

It is hard to take seriously enough the nature of the book as prayer. This sets it off from autobiographies, and answers the principal objections made to it, those having to do with its structure, veracity, and unity.

Structure. Augustine used a patristic Christian scheme of human life to compare the ages of man with the days of Creation and the eras of history (O 2.52–56). There were six of each, and each member in one series reflected the corresponding part of the other two series. Here is the list of them, with the days of Creation placed centrally, since they were the controlling concepts for Augustine (who wrote five extended commentaries on them, including the one in *The Testimony*):

Ages of Man	Creation	History
1. Infantia (pre-verbal)	Light	Adam to Noah
2. Pueritia (speaking)	Sky/Earth	Noah to Abraham
3. Adulescentia (15–30)	Vegetation	Abraham to David
4. Juventus (30–45)	Galaxy	David to Babylon
5. Maturitas (45–60)	Fish	Babylon to Christ
6. Senectus (60–)	Animals/Man	Christ to End

This is not the place to go into all the parallels that stimulated Augustine's imagination over the years. But the first two ages clearly provided the structure for Book One, the work we are considering. What divides and defines these early periods is speech—the lack of it in infancy (*in-fans* means "not speaking," and Augustine plays constantly on that etymology), and the acquiring of it in childhood *(pueritia)*. Day One of the Creation brings an unarticulated light into existence, and Day Two articulates earth and sky by dividing them. In the same way, Augustine has the radiance of being, even as an infant (see *comm.* at **[12]**) and learns to articulate his desires as a child **[13]**. These stages agree with the historical epochs since infancy "is wiped from our memory as by the obliterating Flood" *(Literal Meanings* 1.35), and in the second period the Jews were unable to beget their own people (as Abraham's descendants would, ibid., 36).

The Testimony will clearly mark the point at which Augustine enters the third age (T 2.1), and the fourth age (T 7.1). But since he is still in that fourth stage as he writes, he cannot discuss, as yet, the final two periods. Instead, he anticipates the "seventh day," when God rested on the Sabbath. Since the Sabbath signified, for him and his fellow Christians, the final state after time ends, when the saved soul will contemplate the Trinity, his final three books directly meditate on the days of Creation and their expression of the nature of the Trinity. James O'Donnell has traced the ways trinitarian images run through all the earlier books, with their multiple triads, leading up to the final books' completion (O 2.46–51). In Book One, for instance, the triads of the following passage reflect (a) qualities of the Trinity, followed by (b) distorted images of those qualities pursued in sin, followed by (c) responses to those qualities by the devout: "I sought joy, glory, and truth, not in him but in things he made, in myself and other creatures, thus sliding off toward pain, dejection, and error. Still I thank you, you my delight, my pride, my trust . . ."**[31]**. "Augustine interpreted his life by a textual tradition" (O 2.53).

Veracity. One of the perennial problems in discussion of *The Testimony* is that Augustine "remembers" his life before and soon after his conversion in ways that conflict with the record he left behind in writings from those years. His early letters and reported dialogues give an authentic picture of his intellectual development that he does not even try to reproduce in *The Testimony*, where (for instance) the influence of Neoplatonist teachers like Mallius Theodore is drastically downplayed and the importance of Ambrose vastly exaggerated. But Augustine is not trying to tell us what "really" happened according to our historiographical standards, nor does he want to "clean up" the record in earthly terms. His prayer is a meditation on the action of grace in his life, now acknowledged in ways that he did not always recognize at the time. He is interested in patterns that emerge only in testimony to what God was telling him, despite his resistance or misperception, obstacles from which he is still wrestling free with God's help. For him this is the true story, God's story that he has lived through, moving from blindness toward light. That the pattern corresponds with

God's revelation in Creation and in history just proves that it is grace he is describing, his own participation in the divine drama of salvation.

Unity. The unity of the book—the norms for inclusion and exclusion of material, the progress to a climax in the final three books—becomes obvious once we understand its organizing principle as one of prayer. Augustine does not "all of a sudden" start talking of Genesis and the Trinity in Books Eleven through Thirteen. He has been talking of them all through the earlier books, not only in terms of the days of Creation, but in the way he discusses representative moments. When his father sees him in the baths and knows that he can beget a child (T 2.6), this not only marks the beginning of Augustine's third age *(adulescentia),* capable of procreation. Rather, since he is "clothed" *(indutum)* in nakedness, this recalls Adam's discovery of his own nudity in Genesis, when he felt the need to clothe himself, and it will be contrasted with the spiritual "bath" of baptism by which Augustine heeds the call to be clothed *(induite)* in Christ.

Other events, too, "re-enact" Genesis. The theft of the forbidden pears in Book Two is deliberately recounted in ways that refer to Adam's eating of the forbidden apple—as the dialogue with Monnica in Book Nine, reaching back toward Eden, indicates a partial healing of Augustine's fallen spiritual state. The death of the friend in Book Four makes Augustine compare his envy of the friend's relationship with God to Cain's anger when Abel's sacrifice pleases God. Tracing the presence of many other "Genesis moments" is not necessary here. What matters for Book One is the way the Creation of the whole universe is implicit in the creation of Augustine's petty self—which can, nonetheless, not be called petty because God made and is remaking him—and the way God drew him through the waywardness of boyhood, just as he drew a refractory people through the early books of Jewish Scripture. The unity of the book is the unity Augustine discovers in himself as a reflection of God's unity: "I preserved myself—by an echo of your mysterious oneness, out of which I came to be—as I maintained a single control over everything my senses delivered to me"**[31]**.

3. The Book's Title

Transliterating (rather than translating) *Confessiones* into English as *The Confessions* has the misleading result of suggesting that the book is an autobiography, that Augustine is recounting his sins like someone going into a modern church confessional and spending days there. But confessionals did not exist in Augustine's time, nor anything like the modern sacrament of penance. *Confessio,* moreover, was not primarily self-accusation but any kind of "corroborating" testimony (*con-fiteri* is, etymologically, "to speak with," and Augustine had the rhetorician's love of etymology). Augustine testifies to God as the stars do by their beauty—*pulchritudo eorum confessio eorum* (*Sermon* 241.1). The pagan author Apuleius (also from Africa) said that her jewels "confess" (confirm the status of) the grand dame (*Golden Ass* 2.2). Augustine testifies *(confiteor)* that time is measurable (T 11.33)—one of many uses where sin is not at issue. "The tribes of Israel go up to the Temple to testify *(confiteri)* to God's name" (*Explaining the Psalms* 121.8). Even the devils testify to God's power by their opposition to it (*Interpreting John's Letter* 10.1), as do heretics (ibid., 6.12).

For Augustine, then, testimony *(confessio)* is speech that acknowledges the power and claims of God: "This it is to testify [*confiteri*], to speak out what the heart holds true. If the tongue and the heart are at odds, you are reciting, not testifying" (*Interpreting John's Gospel* 26.2). The proof that *confessio* does not speak only of sin is the fact that the sinless Jesus "confesses" to the Father at Matthew 11.25.

> "I will confess the justice of the Lord" [Psalm 7.18]. This cannot be confessing to sin, since it is said by the one [David as prophetic type of Jesus] who just denied most truthfully that there is "evil in what my hands do" [Psalm 7.3]. This is a testimony to God's justice, the kind that praises God. . . . There can be no admission of sin when the Lord says, "I testify [*confiteor*] to you, Father, Lord of heaven and earth, because you have concealed these things from the learned and revealed them to the lowly [Matthew 11.25]. Ecclesiasticus [39.19–21] puts it the same way: "Testify [*confitemini*] to the Lord for all his works, and your testimony shall make this affirmation: 'All the Lord's works are of the highest good.' " . . . So, after saying "I will testify to the Lord," lest we think he was confessing sin, the

Psalmist adds, at the end, "And I shall sing the Lord's name as the most high." Singing is characterized by joy, not by the sadness sin requires (*Explaining the Psalms* 7.18).

The deepest kind of testimony is the cry of the Spirit in the heart of the believer, drawing a person into the inner conversation of the Trinity. This is the prayer of the Christian community: "As the Spirit gave them an inner testimony to Christ, they spread the testimony themselves" (Sermon 94.2). To *confiteri* is to "speak with" the Spirit to the Father, as well as to speak with a knowledge of one's own willed distance from God in sin. The title of the book thus answers the opening query of the book, how can a mere mortal dare to praise God? He cannot do so unless God himself speaks within the believer through grace and the Spirit. "May my God cry through my soul, your truth assuring me . . ."[22]. One of Augustine's favorite Pauline passages is Romans 10.10: "When the heart believed that we were whole, the mouth testified [*confessionem fecimus*] that we were saved." Though Augustine testifies to his sinful state, he testifies to much else in the book he called a testimony.

4. The Book's Style

The style of *The Testimony* is extraordinarily intimate, a quality derived from its prayer form. Augustine is not preaching outward to others, praising or reproaching them, arguing with any human audience. He is allowing others to eavesdrop on his inner colloquy with God. Because he is praying, he uses the invocations he knows best and uses most, not only in public liturgies but in his private meditations. Scripture phrases are woven throughout his language, not interrupting it but serving as a remembered music that plays along with and through his deepest expressions of emotion. It is hard to indicate the extent of this reliance on Scripture verses without suggesting a chopped-up text. I indicate the most recognizable lines with single quotation marks in my translation, but this should not draw attention away from the flow of words that seamlessly incorporates all biblical echoes.

In this respect, the normal punctuation of the text observed in translations can be inadequate to the stream of consciousness that Augustine achieves, to the long-breathing arcs of his prayer. He often uses a phrase at or near the beginning of such an arc, and then echoes it toward the close. Such members should not be put in different sentences, as Chadwick does in his creditable translation. Thus he translates the second sentence in the opening paragraph of Book One as two sentences:

> Man, a little piece of your creation, desires to praise you, a human 'bearing his mortality with him,' carrying with him the witness of sin, and the witness that you 'resist the proud.' Nevertheless, to praise you is the desire of man, a little piece of your creation.

Augustine is not so choppy:

Yet man, a mere segment of what you made, strives to appraise you—man, 'confined by a nature that must die,' confined by this evidence of his sin, the evidence that you rebuff the overweening, yet man would still appraise you, this mere segment of what you made.

When Augustine launches a thought with a phrase and then repeats it to round off the thought, the unity of movement should be preserved. Here is Chadwick, using five sentences:

Who reminds me of the sin of my infancy? For 'none is pure from sin before you, not even an infant of one day upon the earth.' Who reminds me? Any tiny child now, for I see in that child what I do not remember in myself. What sin did I then have?

This is all one question:

Who is there to remind me of my sin before I spoke?—'no one being clear of sin, not a speechless child with but a day upon this earth'—who will remind me, will any (even the tiniest) baby help me observe what I do not remember myself, will it show me what sin I was committing at that age? [11].

The biblical text Augustine uses most often—the ostinato to his prayer—is the Book of Psalms. The psalms were the staple of church services he presided over—they were used in hymns, readings, and sermons, ready at hand in Augustine's memory to be quoted, paraphrased, or alluded to. They are admirably suited to the prayer form of *The Testimony*. The unit of verse in Hebrew poetry is the couplet that states a theme in two different ways:

> Great is the Lord's power to act
> and his knowing goes beyond measure [Psalm 146.2].

These sighing replications are the overlapping units that determine much of the rhythm of thought in Augustine's prayer. And such couplets are a perfect bridge to the rhetorical devices that were second nature to Augustine, which also moved in doublets—antithesis, chiastic pairs, isocolons, and similar devices: You "honor debts without owing, cancel debts without losing"[4].

5. The Book's Imagery

The Bible also encouraged Augustine to think in images. For him, God is fountain, light, vine, cup of plenty, bread, sky, and other concrete symbols. He knew that God is knowable only in veiled approximations and paradoxical formulations. Though Scripture calls him an angry and a jealous God, Augustine cautions that these are economical expressions suited to human limits. He must add, therefore, that God is "loving, yet not inflamed; jealous, yet not disturbed; regretful, without remorse; angry, without intemperance"[4]. All these are images, not the reality—though they are as close as we can come to certain aspects of reality. The habit of using images is so strong with Augustine that when he uses a symbolic term, it often colors the whole passage where he made it explicit. When Job's language of challenging God to a trial is renounced at [5], Augustine nonetheless goes on to talk of pleading before an implied court in the first sentences of [6].

Scriptural imagery opened a vast interior landscape for Augustine, a geography of the soul where the sower sows seeds, rocky soil resists truth, mountains of belief stand firm, seas are swept with peril, paths divagate or plunge downward or climb up. The most common images in Book One are those connected with paths and with water. The path images are probably the most pervasive throughout Augustine's writing. They reach from the Jewish idiom for "paths of righteousness" and "by-paths of the wicked" to the New Testament message that "I am Path, and Truth, and Life" (John 14.6). Christianity itself is "the Path" in Acts of the Apostles. Augustine associates the Neoplatonic path down from the One and the path back up to It with the prodigal son's travel away from his father and his return [28]. In Book One, he equates moral wanderings from God's straight path with Aeneas's "strayings"[22]. All dark and tangled and thicket-obstructed ways are images of his psychic aberrations: "You drew me from my vicious bypaths, outdazzling with your allure the attractions that misled me, so that I may love you more worthily, hang on to your hand with a whole heart's energy, as you 'carry me out of trial to the final goal' "[24].

The other common image is of water—the stormy seas of worldly converse [13], the wild waves of temptation [18], the stream of Society [26] which one must ride over on the plank of the Cross, the dissolving waters at odds with the shaping waters of baptism.

Perhaps the most important image used in Book One is the treatment of language as an act of mental parturition. This reflects Augustine's rejection of the idea that the mind is a passive tabula on which external things are printed. Book One anticipates aspects of Noam Chomsky's "generative grammar." This generative power is, for Augustine, the action of God within the mind, "the vital principle breeding depth of thought out of my intelligence"[21]. "I went into labor to deliver my thoughts . . . and in their ears I completed the parturition of what I felt within me"[23]. This generation, of course, reflects God's fertile action within the child, "the power that breeds depth of thought out of my intelligence"[21].

6. The Book's Rhetoric

Though Augustine knows how little human language can do to reach God, he does not therefore abandon the rhetorical skills he had acquired so painstakingly. Only the best is good enough for God, however inadequate it might be. We should stretch ourselves, to the extent of our ability, to express our yearning and need for him [4]. No one could be more scathing than Augustine in attacking rhetoric as "phrase peddling" [22] for gain or flattery or seduction. But he did not have the modern prejudice that artful language is of necessity insincere or nonauthentic language. He knew that Scripture itself is highly artful, full of poetry, imagery, antithesis, and paradox. Some of these devices are essential to religious speech itself—God can only be approached by way of paradox and image. The couplet form of the Psalms and other poems is built on antithesis, and tends toward the balancing of speech members *(cola)*.

Antithesis. This, says Gilliam Clark, "is Augustine's favorite technique, if 'technique' is the right word: antithesis is so frequent in all his writing that it seems rather to be the way he thinks." One of the most important antitheses for him is *intus-foris,* "within-without," deployed through Book One as through all his thought. God and the self are within. The world and others are without. Language is the bridge between the two, capable of enriching what is *intus* or of dispersing it. The infant ("pre-verbal") thrashes about to find words for his demands because those without cannot otherwise perceive what is within him. Other regular antitheses are those of God and creature, soul and body, word and act, their elements chiming against each other on every page.

Chiasmus. A special form of antithesis—antithesis compounded, as it were, and "criss-crossed"—is that which bunches two identical elements in the middle and puts two others on the outside. One might print the former in capitals to bring out the construction. A simple case is at **[13]**, describing the ramble-scramble of a child's futile attempts at communication—"my *noises* RANDOM and RANDOM

flailing" (vocibus VARIIS et VARIIS membrorum motibus).
More complex patterns show up constantly: "so long as he
finds in love what he does not FIGURE OUT, instead of FIG-
URING IT OUT without *finding* you"**[10]**. Augustine discovered this figure everywhere in the Psalms.

> I have *sought* your COUNTENANCE,
>
> it is your COUNTENANCE, Lord, I shall *seek* **[28]**.

Paradox. Since God does not fit into our minds or words or
categories, the proper way to speak of him is in contraven-
tion of our categories—as in the long string of paradoxes in
[4]. But the allure of false values is also expressed in paradoxes throughout the book—"this dying life, or should I
call it living death"**[7]**, "to sate insatiable yearnings for
penurious wealth and infamous fame"**[19]**.

Alliteration. The patterning of consonants gives point to
epigrams or satirical definitions. When Augustine says that
a violent baby is *tantillus puer et tantus peccator* **[19]**, it is
not enough to translate (as Chadwick does) "so tiny a child,
so great a sinner," since the interlocking *t* and *p* give a bite of
self-satire to the paradox. We need similarly interwoven
consonants in English: "little in size, large in sin." Again,
when he writes *conturbata matris carnis meae* **[17]**, the
folding in of the sounds on each other, expressing the ma-
ternal bond, demands something like "the mournful bearer
of my mortal body." The play of sounds in *pauca quae
poteram qualia poteram* **[8]** calls for "the best of my little

(and little availing) ability." Alliteration often adds point to other rhetorical devices, as with *vocibus VARIIS et VARIIS* in the chiasmus mentioned above.

Polyptoton. A figure that comes easily to inflected languages is the juxtaposition of the same word in various cases or forms—*misericors misero,* "merciful to me needing mercy"[9], *mecum meorum meaque diligentia,* "care be taken of myself by me and mine"[18]. Or: *miserius misero non miserante,* "more pitiful than a pitiable man without pity"[21]. The play on strategically placed *omnia* and *omnibus* in [13], backed up by the chiming *valerem . . . volebam . . . volebam,* makes fun of the baby's demand for instant wish fulfillment. So *nec valerem quae volebam nec quibus volebam omnibus* should be: "for want of getting each thing I wanted from each person I wanted."

Colometry. Much of the power of Augustine's flow of language comes from the artful varying of the lengths of his sentences' members *(cola).* A good example is the interplay of various grammatical structures and phrase lengths in the tour-de-force sentence on God at [4]. This ranges from climactically lengthening the members to interjecting *isocola* (exactly equal phrases): *reddis debita nulla debens, donas debita nulla perdens* is not only an isocolon, but a paradox involving alliteration and homoeoteleuton (similar endings to successive cola). Thus: "honor debts without owing, cancel debts without losing." The tricolon at [9] rises to a crescendo: with God are "the certain causes of contingent outcomes, the unchanging origins that abide through all that changes, the eternal rationale of all irrational things that pass away." The way God endows a baby with its faculties has the same effect [12]: "how you articulate its sensory apparatus; fit limb to limb, giving beauty to its form; and coordinate all its instincts of self-preservation as a single thing." The interrelationship of verbal technique and theology comes out when repeated tricola refer to aspects of the Trinity.

7. Translating the Book

It will be seen from the above examples that I think the form and force of Augustine's language should be replicated, so far as possible, in an English translation. This is often neglected in translations of prose, though some effort is made to give the effect of form when translating poetry. Augustine's language is as highly wrought a thing as many poems. It is very much aware of its own artistic aspirations. His training as a rhetorician made this inevitable. His skill at turning this secular discipline to sacred uses makes his text dramatic. A translator's aim should be to find some English way of approximating *what* he was saying and *how* he was saying it.

One must be careful, of course, when searching for the modern *way* to say what Augustine said, to retain *what* he said. One might argue, for instance, that if he were alive today he would use gender-neutral language. Maybe, but only if living now made him change his mind about male primacy, and not just the form of his expression. We cannot "educate" him to our values, but must keep to the historical limits of his outlook. Thus "he" will embrace the whole race in this translation. In the same way, we cannot attribute to him less idiosyncratic theories of physical sensation [12], or the language of modern science. Even when he sounds most modern, as in his view of newborn children's mental activity, that cannot be divorced from the theological rationale that underlay his view—i.e., the way the mind (he held) reflects God's generation of the Verbum in the Trinity. Nor can his theology—e.g., on sin, hell, and the devil—be softened to fit modern tastes. It is his whole world that must be brought over into our tongue.

At times Augustine plays so constantly on the etymology of a word that this must be kept foremost in the translation. He was always aware for instance of the literal meaning of *in-fans*, "non-speaking." This led him in his Christmas sermons to pun on the fact that the Christ child was also the Word of God—an "infant Verbum," a wordless Word. So I use "the speechless stage," not "infancy," throughout the translation—which is clumsy, but less so than parentheses pointing up the sense wherever needed.

Problems of tone arise constantly. Augustine's language can be racy, but his attitude is reverent in this long prayer. Self-abnegation should not become bathos. Satire should not become undignified. When he uses a diminutive like *mulierculae* ("little women") of his nurses considered us witnesses, the dismissive note should be struck, but not exaggerated. I call them "gossips" where Henry Chadwick gives us "weak women." It is not lack of strength that is being singled out, but lack of authority as witnesses. Chadwick translates the same word simply as "wives" at T 6.24, where the diminutive means something more like "homebodies" in their opposition to a philosophical commune (see *comm.* [10]). When searching for the right word in an author with the self-conscious artistry of Augustine, the shading of each word, the weighting of it, must be taken into account.

PART II

The Testimony: Book One

Notes

L1 *vast]* Psalm 47.2: "Vast is the Lord, and to be praised as such." *Valde* is "as strongly," i.e., validly, appropriately, as opposed to the Vulgate *nimis* (excessively). Vast is quantitative here, not qualitative, setting up the "size" comparison between Augustine and the Lord *(comm.).*

L2 *what you do]* *Virtus* is Augustine's principle of action.

L2 *beyond assaying]* Psalm 146.5: "Great is the Lord's power to act, his knowing goes beyond measure [*numerus*]." *Numerus* was associated by Augustine with the Second Person of the Trinity (the Verbum), the principle of form *(comm.).*

L3 *strives to appraise]* Man is trying *(vult)* to do what he cannot adequately do. To praise is to fit the right approbation to its object, as part of the language of adequacy throughout this passage *(comm.).* In English, both "praise" and "appraise" mean to "set a price on." The point here is that God is priceless.

L4 *confined]* 2 Corinthians 4.10: "moving within his mortality." This movable prison inhibits the effort to praise God adequately.

L5 *rebuff]* Proverbs 3.34: "God rebuffs the overweening, but favors the lowly."

L8 *tilted toward you]* For Augustine's cosmology of "gravitation" in this passage, see *comm.*

L15 *how shall people call]* Romans 10.13–14: "Who calls on the Lord will be saved—but how can they call on one they do not recognize; how recognize without hearing of him; how hear without being told, and who will tell unless sent to do so?" *(comm.).*

L19 *seeking him they find]* Matthew 7.7: "Seek and you will find."

I. How to Begin?

1. 'Vast are you, Lord, and as vast should be your praise'—
'vast what you do; what you know beyond assaying.' Yet man,
a mere segment of what you made, strives to appraise you—
man, 'confined by a nature that must die,' confined by this evidence of his sin, the evidence that you rebuff the overweening,
yet man would still appraise you, this mere segment of what
you made. You prompt us yourself to find satisfaction in appraising you, since you made us tilted toward you, and our
heart is unstable until stabilized in you.

Then help me, Lord, to recognize and understand what
comes first, to call for you before appraising you, or to recognize you before calling for you. Yet how can one call for what
one does not recognize? Without such recognition, one could
be calling for something else. Or is calling for you itself the
way to recognize you? Yes, 'how shall people call for one they
do not believe exists? And how are they to believe it exists if
no one proclaims it?'

Still, 'those who seek the Lord shall appraise him,' for by
seeking him they find, and by finding they appraise. I shall seek
you then, Lord, by calling for you, call for you by believing you
exist; for you have been proclaimed to us, and it is my belief in
you that calls out to you—the faith that is your gift to me,

L1 *by the humanity]* By the descent to humble station *(humilitatem),* with reference to Philippians 2.7–8.

L2 *mission of proclaiming]* The previous clause shows that the bringing of the good news was a concomitant of the Incarnation. God's Word is the one teacher/preacher. See *The Teacher.*

L11 *has no claim]* Taking *inferi* as possessive genitive, "I do not belong to it."

L12 *if I do go down]* Psalm 138.8: "Go I down to hell, yet there are you."

L15 *from whom]* Romans 11.36: "From him, through him, in him are all things."

L19 *God who has said, 'I fill . . .']* Joel 2.23, 24: "The heavens I fill, and the earth."

L27 *Spirit is poured]* Acts 2.17: "My Spirit over all flesh shall be poured out."

which you breathed into me by the humanity your Son assumed, taking up his mission of proclaiming you.

2.   Yet how shall I call for my God, the God who is my Lord, when it is precisely to me I am calling him when I call, and what in me is large enough for God to enter? How can he who made heaven and earth come into me? Is there anything in me that can hold you? Can even heaven and earth, which you made, and in which you made me, hold you? Or, since nothing that is can exist without you, do all things that exist hold you?

And since I too exist, how can I ask you to come to me, who would not exist if you were not already in me? Hell has no claim on me, not yet; and even there, you are present—so 'if I *do* go down to hell, there are you.' Thus I would not exist, my God, could not exist at all, were you not already in me. Rather, I could not be, were I not in you, 'from whom, through whom, in whom are all things.' Assuredly that is so, Lord, that is so.

Where *to* can I, already in you, call you to come? And where *from* would you be coming? Where *to* could I retire, outside heaven and earth, for God to come there to me, my God who has said, 'I fill heaven and earth'?   3.   Since, then, you fill heaven and earth, do they contain you? Or do you fill them, with a surplus of you left over, beyond their containing? Then where, once heaven and earth are filled, does the overflow of you go? Do you, who contain all things, need no container because what you fill is filled by your containing *it*? Any receptacle containing you cannot confine you—were it broken, you would not spill out of it. When your Spirit is poured out upon us, you do not fall down but lift up, you are not scattered out, but gather in.

L8 *What other Lord]*   Psalm 17.32: "For who is God but the Lord, and who is God but our God?"

L10 *hidden far]*   Augustine, *City of God* 1.29: "God at our side in hiding— yet, without moving, remote."

L13 *age the proud]*   Job 9.5: "who ages mountains away insensibly."

L16 *jealous]*   Joel 2.18: "the Lord is a jealous Lord." Augustine is countering Manichaean criticism of the Jewish Scriptures as attributing unworthy acts and feelings to God, who is said to feel these emotions by analogy with human reactions, though they are not strictly true of him.

L17 *regretful]*   Genesis 6.6–7: "The Lord regretted his making man."

L17 *angry]*   Exodus 4.14: "The Lord was angry at Moses."

L26 *say the most]*   Here and elsewhere in Augustine, *loquaces* are Manichaeans quick to criticize. He called himself, in his Manichaean days, "inflated and verbose in the debates of so-called scholars" (*The Need to Believe* 2); *(comm.)*.

L27 *find stability]*   *adquiescere,* a reference back to the unstable *(inquietum)* heart of **[1]**.

L28 *make it drunk]*   Ambrose, Hymn 1.7.23–26: "Drink we in joy, soberly drunk in the Spirit." *Testimony* 5.23: "soberly drunk on your Vine."

But in filling all things, do you fill them with all of you? Or since all things cannot hold all of you, do they each hold its own part of you—all of them the same part, or each its own part, larger or smaller as they are large or small? Can there, then, be a larger or smaller part of you? Are you not entire everywhere, though nothing can hold the entire you?

4. Then what are you, God—what, I inquire, but simply God the Lord? 'What other Lord is Lord, what other God but God?'—highest, best, most powerful, all-powerfulest, most merciful yet most just, hidden far away yet very near, most beautiful yet most strong, most fixed yet most elusive, changeless in changing all things; neither young nor old, you give youth back to all things yet 'age the proud away insensibly'; active always, always at rest, you acquire without lacking, you support, fill, and protect; create, raise, and complete; seeking, though you have all; loving, yet not inflamed; jealous, yet not disturbed; regretful, without remorse; angry, without intemperance; you change event without a change of plan; acquiring what is at hand without having lost; never in need, yet happy at gain; receiving, without exacting interest on what is owed you; overpaid to be put in debt, yet none pay you with anything you did not, in the first place, give; you honor debts without owing, cancel debts without losing. And what, with all this, have I said, my God, my life holy and sweet to me, what can anyone say when speaking of you? Yet we must say something when those who say the most are saying nothing.

5. Who will help me find stability in you, help you come into my heart, to make it drunk with you, oblivious of my ills

L8 *I am your rescue*] Psalm 34.3: "Tell my soul, 'I am your rescue.' "

L11 *Hide not*] Psalm 26.9: "Hide not your countenance from me."

L11 *die into you*] Colossians 3.3: "For you have died, and your life is hidden away with Christ in God."

L13 *too cramped*] Isaiah 49.20: "Too cramped is this place, make it wide enough for me to dwell in it." Augustine in his commentary on Psalm 100.4: "Our inner dwelling place is our heart."

L16 *inmost sins*] Psalm 18.13–14: "Who knows his own sins? From my own secret acts cleanse me, and save your servant from others." The interpretation of this verse in the translation is taken from Augustine's consistent statements of its meaning—e.g., in *Free Will* 3.29: "Sin has two springs, one from one's own conception, the other from external persuasion."

L19 *anticipated*] *Pro-locutus sum.*

L19 *freed my heart*] Psalm 31.5: "You have freed me of sin's iniquity."

L20 *take you into court*] Jeremiah 2.29: "Would you contend with me in court?"

L21 *iniquity*] Psalm 26.12: "Iniquity is lying to itself."

L22 *If you arraign*] Psalm 129.3: "If you keep record of our crimes, Lord—Lord, who will stand cleared? Do not take your servant to court, since no one alive can be acquitted under your scrutiny."

L25 *earth and ash*] Genesis 18.27: "Shall I, a thing of earth and ash, address my Lord?"

L27 *mock me*] Psalm 2.4: "With laughter from his heavens he will mock them."

and hugging all my good to me, the good you are? Why do you matter so much to me?—pity me enough to let me say. Why, indeed, do I matter so much to you that my loving you is something you require, that you should be angry and threaten me with heavy punishments if I love not? Then can my not loving you be a slight thing? No, it cannot, to my sorrow! Tell me by your acts of mercy, God my Lord, what you are to me. Tell my soul, 'I am your rescue.' Tell me in a way that I may hear. My heart is all ears for it, Lord. Open them and tell my soul, 'I am your rescue.' I shall rush toward those words and lay hold on them. 'Hide not your countenance from me.' Let me die into you lest I die away from your countenance.

6.   My soul is 'too cramped for you to enter it—widen it out.' It is in disrepair—restore it. It is filthy in your sight, I admit and recognize this, but who is to sanitize it? To whom before you should I call out, 'Cleanse me of my inmost sins, and outward promptings fend off from your servant'? I believe in you and that is why, you know Lord, I address you. Have I not anticipated accusation of my own sins, 'and you freed my heart of impiety'? I do not 'take you into court,' you who are Truth. I would not deceive myself, not let 'my iniquity tell itself a lie,' so I go not to court with you. 'If you arraign our sins, Lord— Lord, who can stand the indictment'?

7.   Yet let me enter my appeal before your mercy, let me, 'a thing of earth and ash,' appeal to you, since I enter my plea before your mercy, not before a fellow man, who might well mock me. Or do you, in fact, mock me? But even if you do, you will change your mood and pity me.

L19 *inner and outer*]   Augustine's usual distinction between *intus* and *foris*. God's activity informs not only Augustine's weighing of what the senses deliver to his internal forum, but the initial sensing itself. This is a first sounding of the theme that he learns only from God, even as a struggling infant.

L22 *began to smile*]   Virgil, *Eclogues* 4.60. *Incipe, parve puer, risu cognoscere matrem.* "Smile early knowledge at your mother, child."

II. In-Fans (Speechless)

What would I plead with you, Lord, but my ignorance of whence I came into this dying life, or should I call it living death? I know not whence I came, only that your merciful sustenance kept me alive when I did, as I learned from the parents who gave me flesh—the father from whom, the mother in whom, you made me (but not my memory) begin in time. It was your sustenance I drew from fleshly milk, since neither my mother nor nurses were filling their own breasts with it. You yourself dispensed this baby food through them, following the pattern, the gracious providence, you have embedded deep in nature. You provided that I should wish for no more than was supplied, and that those supplying it should wish to give me what you gave them. The wish to supply me came from the natural instinct you planted deep in them, so that doing me good did them good, a good they did not provide themselves but passed on from you, the source of all good, my God, my rescue at every stage.

This I came to reflect on only later, heeding the persistent call you issued through the inner and outer faculties you blessed me with, but then I knew only how to suck, to sleep when soothed, to cry when my body vexed me—this I knew, no more. 8. In time I began to smile, only in my sleep at first,

L6 *inside me]* The persistent contrast of *intus* and *foris.*

L8 *signal out]* Using "signs something like what I desired." The interplay of body language and the verbal system is a key to Augustine's analysis of children's learning in *The Teacher.* The infant is trying to use a body language it understands imperfectly in order to create its own verbal language *(comm.).*

L21 *causes ... origins ... rationale]* The key terms in a climactic tricolon (Introduction).

L23 *rationale]* For Augustine, God's fixed forms *(rationes eternae)* caused the unfolding forms *(rationes seminales)* of temporal succession.

and later when awake—so it was said of me, and I believed it, since we observe the same thing in other babies, though I do not remember it of myself. Gradually I became aware of my surroundings, and wished to express my demands to those who could comply with them; but I could not, since the demands were inside me, and outside were their fulfillers, who had no faculty for entering my mind. So I worked my limbs and voice energetically, trying to signal out something like my demands, to the best of my little (and little availing) ability. Then, when I was frustrated—because I was not understood or was demanding something harmful—I threw a tantrum because adults did not obey a child, free people were not my slaves. So I inflicted on them my revenge of wailing. I have learned that babies act this way, from the ones I had occasion to observe, who, without having known me [as an infant], taught me more about myself than the nurses who did know me.

9.   See then how I lived on when my speechless stage had died away—unlike you, who live on always, with nothing of you dying away, since before all ages began, before everything that can be called before, you are, and are the God and Lord of all that you created, and in you are the certain causes of contingent outcomes, the unchanging origins that abide through all that changes, the eternal rationale for all irrational things that pass away.

Tell me, your supplicant, Lord, merciful to one needing mercy, tell me whether my speechless stage occurred after some other stage of me had died away. Was it just the time I spent in my mother's body—for I came to be told of that, too,

L1 *pregnant women]*   He is, of course, referring primarily to his partner's pregnancy with their son, Godsend.

L1 *something before]*   Augustine was an agnostic about the soul's origin, but did not believe in any pre-existence of the soul that evaded solidarity with Adam *(comm.).*

L11 *gossips]*   Diminutive *mulierculae,* stressing the flimsiness of Augustine's evidence for his own earliest existence, not the unworthiness of women *(comm.).*

L12 *existence . . . life . . . signaling]*   an echo of the Trinity—*esse, vivere, intelligere*—in the child's basic gifts.

L22 *years never run out]*   Psalm 101.28: "You are the same, and your years do not run out."

and observed pregnant women myself. But was there something before that, my delight, my God? Was I, anywhere, anyone? I have no one who might tell me that—neither father nor mother, nor anyone claiming experience of such a stage, nor any memory of my own. Or do you smile, to mock me as I ask, you who tell me to praise you for what I know, and testify to that? 10. I can bear you testimony, Lord of heaven and earth, returning praise to you for my origin and speechless days, though I remember it not, because you let man learn of his infancy from analogy with other infants, if not from women gossips who were there.

[So even without remembering] I was already in existence and had life, and I was striving, while still (just barely) speechless, to find a way of signaling my own meanings out to others. Where could such a creature come from, Lord, but you? Can any such have framed itself, or found a conduit through which existence and life could stream into him from some other source than you, for whom existing is not one thing, living another, since you are perfect existence, perfect life? Perfect you are, beyond all change, and today does not reach its end in you, yet it does end in you, since all days are in you, nor could they have a course of transit not defined by you. But your years never run out, your years are a single today; and our days, no matter how many—not only our own but those of all before us—run their course through your today, are brought into being in it, find their identity in it; and days still to come shall run their course through it, with their own being and identity, while you alone are identical with yourself, so every tomorrow l.6 *sad for sinner*]   Isaiah 1.4: "How sad it is for a sinning race of men, a people deep in iniquity."

l.9 *no one being clean*]   Job 14.4–5: "Who can be clean of all foulness? Not a single one, so long as he shall live a single day on earth."

l.27 *flailing away*]   The child's desperation to speak was repeated, for Augustine, when he came back to the church desperate for truth: "Dehydrated and weakened by lack of nourishment, I sought the church's breasts with a wild abandon, flailing at them with deep sobs and groans, wringing out a flow that would restore me from my plight" (*The Need to Believe* 2).

to come, every yesterday gone, is made in your today. What does it matter if one fails to figure this out? Let such a one be content to say, "How could this be?"—so long as he finds in love what he does not figure out, instead of figuring it out without finding you.

11. Pay me heed, God. When one says "How sad it is for the sinner," God takes pity, since he made the sinner (without making the sin). Who is there to remind me of my sin before I spoke?—'no one being clean of sin, not a speechless child with but a day upon this earth'—who will remind me, will any (even the tiniest) baby serve for me to observe what I do not remember of myself, will it show me what sin I was committing at that age? Was it sin to work my mouth toward the nipple as I cried? If I did that now, working my mouth not toward the nipple but after food proper to my present state, I would be derided and properly reproached. But though my behavior then deserved reproach, I would not have understood if anyone issued it, the reproach would have had no effect, either from social pressure or personal acceptance. As we grow up, we root out and relinquish such behavior. (People, I observe, when sorting out bad things to reject, do not knowingly throw out the good instead.)

Or is this behavior allowable in terms of a baby's age—to demand with tears what would harm it; to throw a tantrum when not obeyed by servants and adults, by his own parents, by any bystanders (however wise) not knuckling under to its whim; flailing away to hurt (if he could) those who dare disobey his own self-harming ukase? The harmlessness of babes

L4 *sudden pallor*]   For a memory of Godsend in this passage, see *comm.*

L14 *sensory apparatus . . . beauty to its form . . . self-preservation*]   An echo of the Trinity in the human body.

L18 *testimony of song*]   Psalm 9.1–2: "Good it is to testify to the Lord, and sing to your name, you most high."

L21 *oneness . . . beauty . . . law*]   Another trinitarian reference.

is in their body's effect, not their mind's intent. With my own
eyes I was a present witness at what we have all observed, a
tiny thing's fierce competitiveness—how, though he could not
speak, he made himself clear by his sudden pallor and the sour
contortion of his features at a rival for the nipple. Mothers and
nurses claim they can check the tantrum by some trick of their
trade, treating as harmless a baby's effort to deprive another of
the one food it depends on, though the milk flows abundantly
for both. We put up with the tantrum, not because it does not
matter, or matters little, but because the baby will grow out of
it—as we see from the fact that no one will put up with such
behavior in an adult.

12.   You God, who are my Lord, give life to the baby when
you give it a body—we see how you articulate its sensory apparatus; fit limb to limb, giving beauty to its form; and coordinate all its instincts for self-preservation as a single thing. It is
your will that I appraise all this, pay you, the highest of things,
my testimony of song to your name, since this in itself, had
you done nothing more for the baby, shows that you are all-
powerful and kind, that no one else could do what you do—
could, from your oneness, give each thing its degree of being;
from your beauty give it shapeliness; from your law give it its
rank in the creation.

Such, Lord, was the period when I was alive though I do not
remember being so, a period for which I have taken on trust
what others told me, or have guessed at my own behavior from
analogy with other babies. However persuasive such analogy
may be, I hesitate to count that period as part of my life in this

l.2 *conceived in evil*] Psalm 50.7: "For I was conceived, you see, in evil, and my mother sheltered a sinful me in her womb."

world, since it is as wrapped in a darkness beyond recall as was the period I spent in my mother's womb—and if 'I was conceived in evil, and my mother sheltered a sinful me in her womb,' where, my God, I ask you, where, my Lord, was I, your servant, ever free from sin? Beyond that I say nothing of a time with which I recall not the faintest connection.

L9 *All by myself]* The emphatic *ego ipse*. Augustine is not excluding *God's* teaching role, of course, as his next words indicate—God gave him the brain he is using "by myself." But the assertion of independence from human teachers is the key to this whole passage, just as it is the central idea of *The Teacher; (comm.).*

L13 *began . . . to pull in]* The manuscripts' variant reading *prensabam*—"I was beginning [imperfect tense] to grab"—is preferable, as the unexpected word *(lectio difficilior),* to a copyist's tamer *pensabam,* "I began to ponder" *(comm.).*

L14 *people named something]* *The Teacher* 33: "When the word [head] was said again and again, I began to take notice of it and to figure out where in conversation it was being used, until I connected the sound with something already familiar to me from sight."

L14 *named something]* Emphasis on *thing*—which led Wittgenstein to think naming things was all that the learning of language involved for Augustine *(comm.).*

L20 *miming actions]* Literally, "motion of other members [than the face]." In *The Teacher,* Augustine finds a whole language in the mime's art.

III. Childhood (Speaking)

13.   What but childhood could I enter by advance beyond my speechless stage? Or is it better to say that childhood entered me, displacing the speechless stage? Yet my speechlessness did not depart—where else could it have gone?—though it was no longer with me. As soon as I began speaking, I could no longer be speechless, but a speaking child. I remember speaking, though I learned only later *how* I came to speak. It was not by the teaching of my elders, arranging words in some prescribed order, as when I learned grammar. All by myself, using the brain you gave me, my God, for want of getting each thing I wanted from each person I wanted, when my screams, my noises random and random flailing of limbs, did not convey the desires within me, I began to use my memory to pull in what I desired. Whenever people named something, and used the same inflections when indicating that thing with their bodies, I would take note and store in memory the fact that they made the same sound when they wanted to indicate that thing. It was clear they wanted to do this from the physical action that is a body language for all humans—facial expressions, glances, or miming actions that, linked with vocal inflections, convey an intention to get or retain, repel or evade something. The words I heard, used in their right way in different grammatical

L2 *wrestling my mouth]*   Modern observers have recorded the way babies try out and master various sounds in their "nonsense" cooings.

L5 *shaped . . . pressures]*   The language system of Society may not be able to give understanding, but it can corrupt the heart, and in that sense "teach" bad ways.

L18 *people who prayed]*   A glimpse of Augustine's boyhood in the context of his local church—he always said he *returned* to the church, rather than discovered it later in life.

L25 *not yielding]*   Literally, "not to my lack of perception." The translation follows Augustine's understanding of Psalm 21.3: "Cry though I will, my God, you heed me not by day, nor answer at night by leading me to false values, not true ones."

settings, and recurring over time, I steadily accumulated and, wrestling my mouth around these sounds, I expressed what I wanted. With these tools for enunciating what I wanted, I plunged deeper into the storm-tossed lives of those around me, where I was shaped by my parents' direction and the pressures of my elders.

14. God, you who are my God, what pitiable things, things that made me ridiculous, did I undergo when the goal marked out for me as a boy was to follow advice that would make me a success, would give me an orator's facility for gaining human fame and a wealth that deludes its slaves. For this was I sent to school and taught grammar; and though I could not see what use there was in that, I was beaten for not being eager in its pursuit—a custom praised by our elders, since men living long ago laid out the painful course we must be forced down, adding more to the work and suffering that was already our lot as sons of Adam.

But I came across, as well, people who prayed to you, and they made me, in my small way, aware of you as a vague high being beyond my sensible experience, one who could, nonetheless, hear me out and bring me help. Thus, even as a child, I ventured on prayer to you as my support, my place of shelter. Tongue-tied words I faltered out, using my small voice with no small intensity, to be spared being beaten in class; and when you did not grant me my prayer (not yielding to my false values), my elders, including my parents, laughed off my beatings, not wishing me ill, though a large and weighty ill the beatings were for me.

L5 *and to laugh*]   The variant *deridens* for *diligens,* since the two groups (martyrs and parents) are compared in terms of their contempt for suffering, not of their love for others *(comm.).* The martyrs have a right to mock, and do not, while the parents have no right to mock, and do.

L8 *lack . . . lack . . . lack*]   *minus . . . minus . . . minus . . . deerat.* The play on various senses of "lack" undercuts the melodrama of comparison between his schoolboy beatings and the martyrs' sufferings. He did not lack a martyr-sized fear, though it arose simply from a lack of study. The beatings could have been avoided, easily, if he had just done his homework.

L14 gain . . . *game*]   The original pun is *nugae . . . negotia.*

15. Is there, Lord, anyone so brave, so resolute from love of you (aside from mere natural obduracy), is there, I say, anyone so steeled by love for you as to make light of the rack and tearing instruments and other tools of torture (things people all over the earth beg with great terror to escape) and to laugh at those stricken with terror at the tortures as much as parents made light of the torments we children underwent from our teachers? I did not lack any of the panic, or lack any desperation in begging to escape blows—though it was only my lack of attention to reading and writing and performing the assignments given me that was to blame. I had no excuse from lack of memory or talent, which you made sufficient for my age; I simply loved games more, and I was disciplined by those who had their own games (since *gain* is the game of adults). So children's games are punished by their elders, and no one gets worked up for the punished, the punishers, or both, unless some calculater of advantage should *approve* my being beaten for a child's games since the games slowed my rapid advance in the education I could use for viler games. Who, in these terms, was worse—my teacher, who writhed with bitter envy when caught in a solecism by a fellow pedant, or I, when I resented losing my ball game to a fellow player?

16. This is not said to deny my sin, Lord, you who both correct and create all things in nature, but can only correct [not create] sins—it was a sin to defy the edicts of my parents and those teachers, since I later put to higher use the education those people, from whatever motive of their own, made me acquire. I did not disobey them to do something better, but from a

L1 *fantastic tales*]   Not pagan myths but, as the surrounding phrases show, tales of athletic glory in the games. Augustine was a fan of sports celebrities, like a modern boy collecting baseball cards—except that the games had an expressly religious aspect in his day, with vestiges of pagan sacrifice. At T 10.57 and *Order in the Universe* 1.25, Augustine admits to his early fascination with the games, one he helped his friend Alypius to overcome (T 8.13).

L12 *taught about the eternal life*]   Another glimpse of the degree to which the boy Augustine was an active participant in his local church, where the priest would seem to have taken the position Augustine later did, urging the baptism of children—which Augustine's mother opposed in any case but imminent death. This is one of the places where Augustine criticizes his mother *(comm.).*

love of games—I longed for lofty triumphs and fantastic tales
that tickled my ears and made them itch for more, making my
eyes sparkle bright and ever brighter with excitement at the
public games, the play of adults. Those who put on such shows
are clothed with a high dignity that parents wish for their children; and they gladly let those children be beaten if attending
shows hinders their education, which can gain for them the status to put on shows themselves. Look on all this, Lord, with a
forgiving eye, and free us now that we call on you, freeing as
well those who do not call yet, that they may call and you may
free them.

17.   Already in my boyhood I was taught about the eternal life promised us through the Lord's lowliness reaching
down to our haughtiness—I was signed already with his cross,
seasoned with his salt, when I left the womb of my mother,
who turned fervently to you. And you saw, Lord, how I, while
still a boy, almost died from a sudden attack of chest fever—
you saw, Lord and guardian, with what emotion and belief,
with what reliance on my own mother and the mother of us all,
your church, I begged for baptism in Christ your son. The
mournful bearer of my mortal body cared more, from her pure
heart's faith in you, to deliver me into eternal life than she had
to bear me into this one. She made quick arrangements for the
rites of my ablution in the saving mysteries, with my testimony to you, Lord Jesus, for forgiveness of my sins. Only,
instantly, I recovered—so my cleansing was put off, on the
assumption that I would surely be tainted as I grew up, and

L20 *myself by me and by mine]* Polyptoton (Introduction), descriptive of all the cares folding in upon the newly baptized child of Augustine's hypothesis.

L24 *my mother . . . preferred]* Relapsing after her panic during his illness.

L25 *waters' workings]* Literally, "in those [waters] by which I would be wrought," *per eos [fluctus] unde formarer.*

L25 *already reshaped]* Literally, "already the prototype" [of a newborn Christian]. Augustine is contrasting the flood of temptation working on his soft clay with the hard shape his clay might have taken from the different waters of baptism.

the taint, after such a cleansing, would be greater and more perilous.

I already had faith, then, as did my mother and all our household, except my father, who, though he was not yet a believer himself, did not deny me the protection of my mother's devotion, that I should believe in Christ. She made it a point to say that you, not he, were my father, my God, and you helped her in this way to prevail over her husband, staying subservient to him though superior to him, since in this she was obeying your demands.

18.   This is my request, God: I would know, if you will let me, why I was put off, why not baptized; was it for my own good to be given free rein to sin for a while, or was I not, in fact, given free rein? Why even now is it everywhere dinned into our ears, when this or that class of men is discussed, that we should "Let him carry on, since he is not yet baptized," when we do not say about physical health, "Let him further damage his body, since he is not yet given his health." How much better would it have been for me to be healed on the spot, so that care might be taken of myself by me and by mine, that the healing given my soul should be preserved in your preserving ways who gave it—how much better indeed. But mighty storm-waves, and many, were foreseen rolling over me after my childhood, and my mother, understanding this, preferred to commit to the waters' workings my unshaped clay rather than a self already reshaped.

L11 *our every hair*]   Matthew 10.30: "a count is kept of every hair on your head."

L13 *so little in size*]   See Introduction for the alliteration.

IV. Schooling

19. Yet even before my testing time as a young man, even in my childhood, I resisted education and despised those pressing it upon me, though they pressed anyway, and good was done me though I myself did no good. I would have learned nothing if it had not been forced on me, and no one deserves credit for what is forced on him, though the thing itself be creditable. Nor did those forcing me deserve any credit, since the credit is all yours, my God. They did not realize—as they forced learning on me to sate insatiable yearnings for penurious wealth and infamous fame—what different uses I would make of it. But you, 'who keep count of our every hair,' put to my use the useless efforts of those forcing me to learn, and used my resistance, which merited the beatings, as a punishment for me, so little in size, so large in sin. Thus you get the credit for those who earned no credit for what they did to me, and I got the punishment I deserved for resisting what they were doing, for what you have decreed is fulfilled when sin becomes the soul's own punishment of itself.

20. Why I loathed Greek lessons, when I was plunged into them at an early age, I have not to this day been able to fathom. I took fondly to Latin, not indeed from my first tutors but from those called teachers of literature. The basic reading,

L3 *fleshly whims]* Literally, "because I was flesh and a wind wandering off and not returning," adapting Psalm 77.39: "He remembered they were flesh, a wind that strays off without returning." Augustine is striking the theme of wandering thoughts that leads into Aeneas's wanderings in the next sentence.

L10 *astray myself]* Augustine's omnipresent path imagery (see Introduction) identifies his own straying with the travels of Aeneas.

L14 *pitiful . . . pitiable . . . pity]* More polyptoton (Introduction), for which the inflected Latin allows greater variety of forms: *miserius misero non miserante.*

L18 *breeding depth of thought]* Literally, "wedding my intellect to the seat [breast] of reflection," in order to produce the intellectual offspring of that reflection, a recurrence to Augustine's striking view of thought as parturition, the generation of an inner *Verbum.* God is the vital principle *(virtus)* working through this cross-fertilization—a variant on Augustine's more normal identification of God as the *light* that makes intellection possible.

L23 *exploring with the sword]* Virgil, *Aeneid* 6.457: "You were dead, having by sword explored your utmost doom."

L25 *to earth returning]* Genesis 3.19: "Sprung of earth, to earth you shall return."

writing, and numbering in Latin I considered as dull and irk-
some as any aspect of my Greek lessons—the explanation of
which must be sin and the aimless life of 'fleshly whims that
stray off without returning.'

Actually, the basic lessons were the more valuable ones, just
because they went by rule, letting me acquire and retain the
ability I still hold to read any book I come across, or to write
exactly what I want to say—things more useful than the strayings of some Aeneas that I was forced to memorize while for-
getting that I was astray myself, better certainly than my tears
for the perished Dido, who killed herself from love, while I, the
truly pitiful one, was dry-eyed to my perishing, my God, from
loss of you.

21.   Who is more pitiful than a pitiable man without pity
for himself—one who weeps for Dido, dead because she loved
Aeneas, but not for himself, dead because he failed to love
you, God, my heart's enlightener, the feeder of my soul's inner
hunger, the vital principle breeding depth of thought out of
my intelligence? I [not Aeneas] was the abandoner, the faith-
less lover, and my faithlessness earned the world's "Bravo!
Bravo!"—since love of the world is abandonment of you, and
the world cries "Bravo! Bravo!" to keep its own in line. For all
this I had no tears, only tears for Dido, 'exploring with the
sword her utmost doom.' So I, in flight from you, explored the
utmost depths of your creation, 'earthy and to earth returning.'
If I had been forbidden to read this tale, I would have lamented
the loss of what made me lament, so crazed are those who think

L8 *veils of honor]* Entry drapes were signs of dignity, for teachers and others. See Augustine's *Sermon* 51.4.5: "The more honored the man inside, the more drapes hang at his house's entry."

L9 *phrase peddlers or purchasers]* *venditores grammaticae vel emptores.* Augustine uses the term "phrase salesman" *(venditor verborum)* to mock his own role as court orator in Milan (T 9.13).

L27 *Creusa herself ghosting]* Virgil, *Aeneid* 2.772: "sad trace of Creusa herself's ghost."

belles lettres nobler than the rudiments of reading and writing I had to learn.

22. Now, however, may my God cry through my soul, your truth assuring me "That is not the case, not at all—basic learning was far better." Assuredly I am readier to forget, now, the strayings of Aeneas and all his sort than to lose my ability to read and write. Ceremonial draperies are hung at the school door, but they are not so much veils of honor for the esoteric as blinds for the erroneous. And let no phrase peddlers or purchasers scorn me, an escapee from their thrall, while I give you my soul's willing testimony, since I accept the correction of my strayings, I long to tread your righteous ways. If I should confront them with the straightforward question whether the poet spoke true when he claimed that Aeneas went to Carthage once upon a time, the uneducated will admit they do not know, while the educated admit it is not true. But if I ask how to spell Aeneas' name, all those who know how to read will give the right answer, honoring the agreed-on conventions that establish the alphabet. Similarly, if I ask what would make life less bearable, to forget how to read or write or to forget those poetic imaginings, we know what anyone in his sound mind will say. So it was sinful of me to prefer airy trifles to the solider rudiments—or, more accurately, to loathe the latter and love the former. The singsong "one and one make two, two and two make four" was detestable to me, but sweet were the visions of absurdity—the wooden horse cargoed with men, Troy in flames, and "Creusa herself ghosting by."

L15 *labor to deliver]* In Augustine's "language obstetrics," the child performs his own mental delivery, using as instruments words not specifically aimed at assisting him (e.g., tutors' conscious instruction), but words encountered "higgledy-piggledy." Using this material, the child is able to deliver the offspring of his brain, expressing his own inmost needs, to the external world (his listeners' ears) *(comm.)*.

L25 *Hear, Lord]* Psalm 60.2: "Hear, Lord, my cry to you."

L28 *vicious bypaths]* One of the most extended uses of Augustine's "path imagery" (Introduction).

23. Then why did I loathe Greek literature, which has tunes for the same kind of tale? Homer knew how to weave the same spells, just as pleasantly trivial, yet he repelled me as a boy. I suppose Greek boys would feel the same about Virgil, if they were forced to con him as I conned Homer. It is hard, very hard, to pick up a foreign language—for me, this dashed with bitterness all the sweet Greek nonsense. I was ignorant of the words, and violent threats and acts were used to make me learn them. Once, admittedly, still in my speechless state, I knew no Latin words either. Yet I applied myself to learning them, without intimidation or coercion, surrounded as I was by nurses who coaxed, adults who laughed, and others fond of playing with a child. The Latin words were learned without others' punitive insistence that I learn. From my own heart's need I went into labor to deliver my thoughts, which I could not have done without a stock of words, picked up not just from tutors but from anyone who spoke with me, and in their ears I completed the parturition of what I felt within me. Unfettered inquisitiveness, it is clear, teaches better than do intimidating assignments—which assignments, nonetheless, chasten random inquisitiveness within rules, your rules, God, imposed even in the beatings of teachers, as in the trials of martyrs, those healing pains that draw us back from the sickly pleasures that might drift us off from you.

24. 'Hear, Lord, my cry to you,' lest my soul prove too weak for your discipline, lest I prove too weak to bear testimony to all your merciful dealings with me, by which you drew me from my vicious bypaths, outdazzling with your

L3 *carry me]* 1 Corinthians 1.8: "He will be your strength all the way to the goal."

allure the attractions that misled me, so that I may love you more worthily, hang on to your hand with a whole heart's energy, as you 'carry me out of trial to the final goal.' You see, Lord, my king and God, I would use whatever I learned as a child for your service, whatever I speak or write or enumerate—since you disciplined me when I was learning trifles, and have forgiven me the sin of taking my delight in them; for I learned some useful words even from trifles (though I might have learned them from less trivial sources, as is the safer way for children to proceed).

L1 *Society]*   *Mos* (Custom) is the personified way life is lived in common, which carries people in a flood of multiplying practices—like the passed-on habit of beating a child, or the "storm" of general conversation at **[13]** or the storm-waves of temptation at **[18]**. Here Augustine moves into the final section of Book One, describing how conformation to the world, thrust upon him by his sinful fellow children of Adam, deformed God's gifts in him.

L4 *the Wood]*   Augustine regularly refers to Christ's cross as a plank to cling to in the flood of human sin (O 2.86).

L8 *gowned]*   Literally, "wearing rhetors' hoods."

L9 *breathes the same court air]*   Literally, "of the same dust" (of the public arena).

L15 *hellish river]*   What Augustine has against the school system is that it sets the patterns of socialization that trap people in blind efforts at respect—a respect to be derived from actions shameful in themselves. Even adultery is not the product of mere lust but of expectations set up by peers and superiors' pressures—the point of the passage on Terence that follows.

V. Conforming to a Deforming Society

25.   Cursed be you, Society, onstreaming—who can stand against your tide never stemmed, your torrent carrying Eve's sons out to the vast sea's peril, where even those who ride on the Wood barely survive? Was it not from you, Society, that I learned how Jove is both thunderer and adulterer? He could not really be both, but he was portrayed as both, so that real adultery could be indulged with fictitious thunder serving as its pimp. What gowned rhetorician can take it seriously when his fellow, who breathes the same court air, says: 'Homer in his fictions made gods behave like humans, but I prefer for humans to behave like gods'? Well, in fact, Homer did create fictions precisely to give divine sanction to human vice, so vice would not seem vicious, and those indulging it could claim to be following the example of gods on high, not of lowliest men.

26.   Into you, you hellish river, men's children are thrown, to learn such things for a price, and a great ceremony is made when they display what they have learned in the forum, the very place where the teachers' state fees, superadded to the private fees, are posted. And the river, pounding against these rocks, roars out: 'This is the reward for learning literature, for acquiring the eloquence needed to plead persuasively and argue well'—as if we could never have encountered the phrases

L2 *Terence*]   In the comedy *The Eunuch* (161 B.C.E.), lines 583–91. The words referred to by Augustine are italicized:

> While she was sitting in her room, she viewed
> A mural in which Jove himself pursued
> A maid, ejaculating *showered gold*
> Into her *lap*—for me, example old
> Of just what I was up to in disguise.
> He too arrived as man, to *trick* her eyes.
> If ev'n this god, who thumps *heaven's temples* so
> With crashing noise, showers also down so low,
> Can lowly I not follow where he goes?
> You bet, and have great fun, too, heaven knows.

Augustine's departures from known texts show that he quotes from schoolboy memory—an example of the tainting of the young mind he is describing.

L14 *choice and precious vessels*]   Acts 9.15: "a vessel of choice." Proverbs 20.15: "a precious vessel."

L25 *fending off*]   Virgil, *Aeneid* 1.38: "Nor can I fend Troy's king from Italy."

'showered gold' or 'lap' or 'trick' or 'heaven's temples,' or other words put together in one place by Terence, if he had not put on stage a vile young man taking Jove as a model for his act of rape. The man gazes on a mural presenting the device by which Jove tricked a woman, ejaculating himself as showered gold into her lap. Just see how the youth works up his lust, as if by heavenly injunction:

> If ev'n this god, who thumps heaven's temples so
> With crashing noise, showers also down so low,
> Can lowly I not follow where he goes?—
> You bet, and have great fun, too, heaven knows.

Vocabulary is surely not acquired more readily by means of obscenity, but *this* vocabulary makes obscene acts more acceptable. I indict not the words, which are 'choice and precious vessels' in themselves, but the wine of error poured into them by teachers drunk with it, who beat us if we do not drink with them, and we cannot appeal to any sober arbiter—not that I did not drink it gladly, my God, I recall that fact clearly before your gaze, I was wretch enough to enjoy it. That, indeed, is why I was said to be a promising child.

27. Let me say, my God, something of the talent, your gift, that I dissipated on various forms of nonsense. I was called to a contest that destabilized my mind between praise hoped for and embarrassment or a beating feared: I had to recite the speech of Juno as she raged in anguish over not 'fending off Troy's king from Italy.' I had learned that no Juno ever said that, but we were compelled to follow poetical strayings into

L7 *drifted smoke*]   Literally, "smoke and wind," like *fama fumi,* "reported smoke" at *The Need to Believe* 36, or *vendere fumum,* "selling smoke" in Martial (4.5.7).

L10 *heart's young tendrils*]   John 15.4: "The tendril bears no fruit if separated from the vine; nor can you if you are separated from me, since I am the vine, you the tendril."

L11 *rotten prey*]   Virgil, *Georgics* 2.60: "The [untended] vine yields only birds' prey of rotten grapes."

L19 *long patient*]   Psalm 85.15: "long patient, very merciful, and true."

L23 *whose heart tells*]   Psalm 26.8–9: "My heart has told you, 'I have sought your countenance, your countenance, Lord, I shall long for.' "

L27 *younger son*]   The parable of the prodigal son, at Luke 15.11–32, is a structural model for *The Testimony* (O 2.95–97); *(comm.)*.

L28 *horses or chariots*]   Plotinus, *The Nines* 1.6.8, describing descent from the One and the need to return to It: "Let us fly back to the homeland . . . by what vehicle of escape? We do not need to walk . . . nor to employ a chariot-and-team, nor any kind of boat." This is a passage often echoed in Augustine, and it ties in with the departure and return of the prodigal son (O 2.95); *(comm.)*.

unreality, paraphrasing in prose what was set down in verse. The child who best adapted the emotions of rage and anguish to the status of the imaginary queen, fitly decking her thoughts out in words, was given the prize.

What of value was it to me, my God, my true life, that my recital was praised beyond the multitude of my fellows in age and study? What was this but drifted smoke? Was there no other way to develop my talent and my speaking voice? Honoring you, giving honor to the words of your scripture, would have 'trellised up my heart's young tendrils,' not raveling them out in vain exercises to be 'the rotten prey of birds.' So many ways we find to honor the dark angels.

28. It is not surprising that I was swept along in folly away from you, my God, and wandered abroad, when the role models I was given were ashamed if they were caught describing their own good behavior in ungraceful or ungrammatical terms, but luxuriated in men's praise if they could describe their vicious acts in choice words well fitted together, flowing with easy and elegant phrases. Do you Lord, 'long patient, very merciful and true,' look on all this in silence? And will your silence never end? Already you are drawing from such an immense abyss the soul that longs for you, that thirsts to be satisfied by you, whose heart tells you, 'I have sought your countenance, it is your countenance, Lord, I shall seek,' for to be far off from your countenance is to be in a murk of feelings. It is not by walking or by any locomotion that one moves off from you or comes back to you the younger son of the parable did not call for 'horses or chariots or ships, nor soar off on

L18 *Treat another*] Matthew 7.12: "Treat another as you would be treated yourself."

L20 *housed on your heights*] Isaiah 33.5: "Lofty is the Lord, housed on heights."

L27 *I, wretch*] The last three paragraphs report the deformation Society wrought upon Augustine's youth, tarnishing the gifts God gave him.

visible wings, nor trudge along on foot,' when in a distant land he prodigally wasted what you, mild father, had given him on departure. Mild when he left, you were milder when he came back destitute. To be in a lustful murk of feeling, therefore, is what being far off from your countenance means.

29. Look on, Lord God, and, as you look, with patience look at how carefully men's sons honor earlier speakers' conventional arrangements of letters and syllables, while they neglect your eternal arrangement for eternal salvation—so that if one who is taught or teaches the rules of speech should, against the norm of pronunciation, drop the *h* before 'human being,' he is more censured by human beings than if he, a human being, should, against your rule of love, hate any other fellow being—as if another human being could hurt him more than does the hate he directs at that human being, or as if a man could inflict on a foe some wound greater than he inflicts on his own heart by letting it hate. The rules of grammar are not as deeply inscribed as the morality of scripture, which says: 'Treat another as you would be treated.' How hidden you are, God, 'housed on your heights,' who alone are great, cloaking in penal darkness all criminal desires, when you look on while a would-be champion orator stands before a judge, with a crowd looking on, and lashes his opponent with a boundless hate, yet is cautious not to say something ungrammatical, like 'between he'—and he does not care that the rhetorical storm he is working up may sweep his victim off from life.

30. I, wretch, was even as a child abandoned to Society, left at the edge of the arena where I was to contend, where I was

L5 *swept off]* Psalm 30.23: "I said in my anguish, 'I am swept off from the gaze of your face.' "

L10 *ludicrous clumsiness]* Literally, "with a ludicrous wobbling [instability, *inquietudine*] to imitate [plays]." The fact that the bias toward plays is a perversion of the imbalance of the *cor inquietum* toward God [1] is underlined by the triad of charms inverting the claims of the Trinity: games-plays-imitate.

L27 *Heaven's kingdom]* Matthew 19.14: "Allow the children to approach me, since heaven's kingdom is for the like of these."

more afraid of committing a solecism than concerned, if I did so, with my envy at any who did *not* commit it. I tell you this, and testify, my God, that this kind of praise was what I sought from those whose approval was my goal in life. I did not realize in what a maelstrom of ugliness 'I was being swept off from your gaze.' What could be fouler than the way I earned disapproval even from the worldly with my endless lies told to pedagogue, to teachers, to parents, so I could indulge my love of games, my passion for trivial plays, for re-enacting them with ludicrous clumsiness.

I also sneaked food from my parents' cupboard or table, to pamper myself or to give to others, who exacted this price for letting me share their delight in the games they played. And, once in the game, I often maneuvered to overcome others by devious means, overcome myself by a blind urge to win—yet I was a stickler for the rules, too, and savagely denounced any other's infraction of them I uncovered, even when it was the very infraction I was guilty of; while if *I* was caught out and denounced, I would throw a fit rather than admit it.

Is this the innocence of children—how can it be, I ask you, Lord, how can it, my God? Is it not a natural progression, from one stage of life to the succeeding ones, to move from playing for nuts and balls and sparrows, under pedagogues and teachers, to playing for gold, estates, and slaves, under governors and kings, and to move from beatings in school to criminal sentences? You, then, praised nothing but a child's small stature, as a symbol of humility, dear king, when you said 'Heaven's kingdom is for the like of these.'

L5 *a single control*]   A return to the mystery of each animate thing's unitary action through all its parts *(comm.)*.

L16 *joy, glory, and truth*]   This first triad goes with the two that immediately succeed it, showing the Trinity under three aspects, as truly seen, as falsely sought, and as rewarding the seeker:

joy	pain	delight
glory	dejection	pride
truth	error	trust

The whole of Book One is implicit in this sentence, which counterpoises the essential goodness of Augustine's self as received from God with the counter-bias of Adam's sin and Society's deformations. The latter tugged him away from God even before he realized how they conscripted him into the world's system of sin.

31.   I must, however, still give thanks to you, Lord, highest and best maker and ruler of this universe, had you given me only the life of a child; for during that time I existed, I experienced sensation, I preserved myself—by an echo of your mysterious oneness, out of which I came to be—as I maintained a single control over everything my senses delivered to me, and my first slight hold upon slight truths gave me satisfaction. I tried to avoid fallacies, my memory developed, I learned to wield words, I was shaped by friendship, I shunned being hurt or losing hope or being fooled. What, in this animate life of mine, was not admirable, worthy of praise? All of these were your gifts, God, I did not endow myself with any of them—and the sum of these good things was myself. My maker is good in himself, and my only good, and I hold him high for all the good that was in me even as a boy. Only sin was my own, when I sought joy, glory, and truth not in him but in things he made, in myself and other creatures, thus sliding off toward pain, dejection, and error. Still I thank you, you my delight, my pride, my trust—I thank you, my God, for your gifts to me, may you preserve them, thus preserving me, so that everything you gave me may grow and be improved, and I shall be with you, whose gift it is that I exist.

PART III

Commentary

⟨❧⟩

I. How to Begin?

1. The originality of Augustine's work is marked from the outset. It is different not only from other people's books, but from his own: "No other work of his begins with direct address to God" (O 2.8). Though that points us in the right direction—that Augustine is writing a prayer, not an autobiography—this exordium is also unlike any normal beginning of prayer in the classical era. Suppliants addressed deity by a title or titles that gave them some specific claim on the god. Diana of Ephesus will hear her clients if (and because) they are Ephesians, or because they come to worship in her cult shrine at Ephesus, or because they share some attribute of her cult (as virgins, for instance, or hunters). Zeus the Protector of Guests (Philoxenos) will avenge wronged guests as a proof his own prerogative. The more titles one can claim as appropriate for one's plea, the greater leverage is exerted on the god.

Was this form of prayer ruled out for Augustine because of its pagan roots? Not quite. The Jewish Scripture he uses speaks in terms of the Covenant to "the God of our fathers," to the God of the Promises made to Abraham and Moses. There is even a trace of such thinking in the New Testament prayer par excellence, which calls on "Our Father" by a double claim, as Father of the Jewish ancestors and as Father of Jesus. Even the prayer's spatial invocation ("the One in the heavens"—*ho en tois ouranois,* Matthew 6.9) supplants reference to cult places by appeal to a trans-cult *place.*

Nothing of that tradition is appropriate for *The Testimony.* The old prayer form approached the god by limiting deity to a place, or a role, or a compact by which it was bound. But Augustine asserts that God is beyond all limit, beyond any obligation we can impose on him, any privilege we can assert. We humans have, in the legal sense, "no standing" with him. We cannot control what we cannot measure, even to praise. This is a prayer that has to forswear everything, even the claims of prayer. So here is the first of the endless paradoxes about *The Testimony:* it is a prayer that does not begin like a prayer. And a second paradox follows immediately: it begins, instead, as that least likely thing for such an intimate (almost private) book— an oration. Though Augustine cannot appeal to a cult title or place or function for his opening, he does turn to the tricks of his own rhetorical profession.

To assert one's *aporia* (paralysis) before an imposing (if not impossible) task, to plead one's shortcomings ("unaccustomed as I am . . ."), to ask for undeserved help from one's audience— that is the classical orator's "preemption of sympathy" *(captatio benevolentiae).* Is such an artificial device, stilted and often insincere, out of place in a prayer addressed to God? It does, at first, seem so. Even while he is saying that he has no claim upon the deity, Augustine uses a topos meant to "captivate" the divine audience, bind it to the speaker. But Augustine makes of the maneuver a startlingly new thing, seeing that what is rigged or hyperbolical when used in the forum, or in human law courts, has a depth of literal meaning when directed at the audience from which Augustine most needs a hearing, but which he can least command. Here is *aporia* indeed—God is *laudabilis,* worthy of praise; but no one is worthy enough to praise him. Augustine avoids the Vulgate reading of the Psalm he quotes in his opening line, though he had used that reading in *Explaining the Psalms* (95.4), where God deserves praise *nimis,* "exceedingly," not *valde,* "strongly [enough]." Since *valde* is simply a contraction of *valide,* it means validly or adequately. It is absurd, in Augustine's view, to think God can be praised excessively, or beyond his merits. He cannot even be praised (by us) inadequately, or below his merits. Though God deserves praise equal to his vastness, we are in no position to deliver it. His wisdom, we are told, is beyond appreciation *(numerus).*

Numerus had a powerful technical (and mystical) meaning for Augustine in just the period when he wrote this opening. Over the years he had already formed his cosmology around a favorite verse in the book of Wisdom (11.21), to which he gave a trinitarian interpretation (O 2.293–95): "You have ordered all things by measure [*mensura*] and number [*numerus*] and weight [*pondus*]." Much as he had cited this line before, he gave it special attention in the years around 400, when he was using it to explore the profundities of the creation narrative in Genesis. That meditation was carried on in three overlapping works of the period, *The Testimony, Literal Meanings in Genesis,* and *The Trinity.* All three terms of the Wisdom verse are used in the opening paragraph of *The Testimony*, where the explicit doctrine of *Literal Meanings* sets the implicit framework of this prayer's opening.

In *Literal Meanings* 4.3–4, Augustine asks whether God is number, and answers that he is not number himself, but is beyond number—just as he is beyond measure and weight. These three principles of order are also principles of limit—limiting, specifically, extension and form and stability. Since God does not have limits, he cannot be ordered by these principles, though he emanates the principles for ordering others. He is Numbering, but not numbered—that is the sense of Augustine's *non est numerus* in the second line of *The Testimony*. God is "Measure without measure, Number without number, and Weight without weight" (*Literal Meanings* 4.3).

What Augustine says in *The Testimony*, quoting Psalm 146, is that God's wisdom *(sapientia)* has no number. Number in these works of ca. 400 is the principle of form, of music, of beauty, of words, as well as of wisdom. It is the way the One is articulated in the many. Computing *numerus* is not at issue here, so much as *appreciating* the principle of beauty and order. Computation belongs better to *mensura*, the first term in the book of Wisdom, which establishes each thing's extent of being. Though *mensura* is not, like *numerus*, expressly mentioned in the opening paragraph of Book One, it is present in the way the text contrasts the vastness of God and his creation with Augustine's own limited segment *(portio)* of the whole. Setting the degrees of existence, the limits of each *portio*, is the act of the creating First Person of the Trinity. Since Augustine is thinking in this context of extent, *Magnus*, the first word of the book, should not be translated "great," since that can refer to nobility or other qualities, while the problem of the opening paragraphs is that there is no match between Augustine's insignificant *portio* in relation to the vastness of God and his creation.

The third term from the Wisdom verse is weight *(pondus)*, which is referred to in these words of *The Testimony*'s first paragraph: "Our heart is unstable [*inquietum*] until stabilized [*donec requiescat*] in you." The ancient principle of "gravity" described each physical thing's "restlessness" so long as it was kept from reaching its natural level in the variously dense texture of the physical world. This natural place was determined by the mixture, in anything, of the aspiring or light elements (fire and air) with the thick or lapsing elements (earth and water). Push oil down in water, it will "gravitate" up, since it has important traces of fire in it. In this system, "weight" does not respond, as in the Newtonian universe, to a uniform drag of everything downward to a center. It manifests multiple pulls of things up, away, or down, to differentiated levels. So in modern terms "weight" is a misleading translation for *pondus*. We are talking of a thing's natural "level." Augustine often referred to this system, spelling it out for his congregation in *Explaining the Psalms* 29.2.10:

> A thing's natural level [*pondus*] is a kind of urgency [*impetus*] making it strive [*conare*] toward its proper place. That is its level. Pick up a stone, you are affected by its natural level. It

presses down on your hand, since it wants to be where it belongs. If you would see what it wants, pull your hand away. It falls to the ground, and is stabilized [*quiescit*] on the ground. It follows its tendency, and finds its proper place. Its level is its unwilled energy [*motus*], without any life or sensation. Other things strive upward. If you pour water over oil, it sinks to the bottom by its own level [*pondere*]. It wants its own place, it wants to be in order with respect to other things, since oil is above water in the order of nature. Until it achieves that order, it has an unstable [*inquietus*] energy. On the contrary, if you pour oil under water—as, let us say, a flask of oil falls overboard into the water, into the ocean or the sea, and breaks—the oil will not just passively lie there. . . .

From analogy with this physical system Augustine creates a psychological gravity of the Spirit as an attractive force drawing souls to their proper level: "My level is my love—wherever I am tugged, it is the thing tugging me" (T 13.10). Augustine wrote in his book *Music*: "Satisfaction [*delectatio*—compare "You prompt us yourself to find satisfaction," *delectet*] is the natural level of the soul. It is what puts the soul in order— 'Where your treasury is, there will your heart be' [Matthew 6.21]." This drag on the heart, this *pondus*, is associated with the Third Person of the Trinity through the third term in Wisdom 11.21. The corruptible human body tends downward, but "our [spiritual] heart is unstable until stabilized in you." This spiritual gravity acts against natural gravity (which the Spirit also establishes in the universe). That is how God has made us biased, or unbalanced, *ad te*.

The whole of Wisdom's cosmological scheme, then, is present in the opening lines of *The Testimony*, dwarfing Augustine, making his effort at prayer seem doomed. He is an insignificant part of a whole he cannot measure, understand, or control. How can he praise, when fitting tribute to its object is an act of appraisal, and God is too great to be appraised? The unknowability of God is brought home to Augustine in the lack of a cult title by which to call on him. There is no ritual beginning of prayer here, no controlling invocation. "How can one call for what one does not recognize?" But where man is helpless, God himself takes the initiative, lowering his own level to man's. The Spirit may make the human heart aspire up, but that is not sufficient unless the Son "ascends down" into the lowliness *(humilitas)* of the Incarnation, turning the whole concept of levels topsy-turvy. The incarnate Son is the Word and the bringer of the Word, the praying human who will make possible a praying humanity, breaking up the *aporia* that paralyzed the whole praying project. Augustine's topos, his *captatio*, cannot really pre-empt the sympathy of his divine audience, but the Son has pre-empted Augustine's call by his antecedent response. The call does not elicit response. In fact, the response is what makes the call possible, grace enabling one to seek for grace.

2. As Augustine has no cult title to call on, he has no cult place, no *pou sto*, no where-to-stand. "Where *to* can I, already in you, call you to come?" Yet paradoxically, while he has no place where he might call God to a meeting, he also has no place where he might escape him, or avoid meeting him—not even if, like the Psalmist, he descends to the abyss. Even there, so long as anything exists, it is as a result of God's existence, and is ordered by its own kind of *mensura, numerus,* and *pondus*. One cannot step away from God in order to face toward him. We are in him, and he in us, "deeper in me than I am in me" (*intimior intimo meo,* T 3.11). We cannot call to us the already there.

3. The mystery of God's continuing act of creation in everything created means that God is everywhere, yet contained nowhere—a circle whose center is everywhere and circumference nowhere. The quandary here is what Augustine described in *Faith and Creed* 7: "God has no opposite. If asked for the opposite of white, we would say black; for the opposite of hot, we would say cold; of swift, slow; and so on. But if asked for the opposite of What Is, we can only answer: what is not." The *aporia* just deepens: God is both too far from Augustine and too close to be addressed—too high above, and too deep within. No wonder this prayer opens with a string of unanswerable questions.

4. Augustine has admitted that there is no cult title that compels or even identifies God—"what are you, God—what,

I inquire, but simply God the Lord?" (a question, not an invocation). But then he gives a series of "titles" that are self-canceling, paradoxes that state what God is not. He takes a series of terms from Scripture that are obviously not true in a literal sense. These are the very terms that had led him to mock Jewish Scripture in his Manichaean days (T 3.13–18), and he told Manichaeans after his conversion that orthodox Christians did not take them literally: "The object of our religion is not a God who repents, who is jealous, needy, or cruel, who takes delight in the sacrifice of human or animal blood" (*Catholics' and Manichaeans' Moral Codes* 1.10.16). Yet the terms are undoubtedly present in Scripture, so God must have wanted them there. Augustine says they are the half of a paradox that we must complete: "loving, *yet* not inflamed; jealous, *yet* not disturbed; regretful, *without* remorse; angry, *without* intemperance." These are what Newman called "economies"— ways of moving us closer to the truth without being able literally to state it. Terms like "father" and "son" are not literally true of the Trinity, but are paradoxes of this sort: "Father, *yet* not pre-existing his 'offspring'; Son, *yet* coeval with his 'sire.' " Paradox is a way of knowing by admitting what you do not know.

O'Donnell thinks that the Manichaean objection to these terms is what leads Augustine to end the paragraph with a swipe at *loquaces* (a nice frog-croak of a word)—"those who say the most" while meaning the least. He describes one Manichaean controversialist as "one who, to put it gently, has given the slightest consideration to the things he most likes to talk about" (*The Pragmatism of Belief* 3). But in adding that everyone must say something about God, Augustine is denying that there is an intellectual "means test" for praying to God. We must pray as best we can; but we are all, even the most sophisticated, using baby talk when we speak of God.

5.   This paragraph "unpacks" the last sentence of the preceding one, where it was asserted that we *must* speak of and to God. He requires it without "needing" it, by a gratuitous entry into a relationship of love with us, one that we can reject but not ignore. It is literally a "life or death" matter to us. If we deny that love, we die to its rich world; and bodily death is nothing compared with that. Augustine, *Sermon* 231.3.3: "One who has not died and risen [in Christ] may live on but he lives evilly—and if evilly, not really living. Let him die, lest he die. How can he die lest he die? By undergoing conversion lest he undergo damnation."

6.   By admitting his unworthiness even to pray, Augustine "throws himself on the mercy of the court." He has admitted the indictment before it is served *(pro-locutus sum)*.

II. In-Fans (Speechless)

7. For Augustine, the in-fans, the non-speaker, is a mystery. He cannot remember being one, and of course he left no spoken words from his time as a non-speaker. Since memory and language are, for him, the intertwined principles of identity, how can he say that he had any identity that is unremembered and unspeaking, that *that* he was really he? Memory is the link between the present instant and every lived instant that preceded it. Break that link, and what continuity can there be with a former self, one known only from others' reports (gossips in his nursery) or from the supposition that he must have been what other infants seem to be? Furthermore, language was formed by the use of memory [8]—that is one reason the in-fans does not speak—and remembered things are often summoned up in connection with words (*Teacher* 1). Take away both memory and language, and Augustine finds no difference between the infant state and the time he spent in the womb—or even some earlier time than that, if there was one [9].

Augustine will say in [13] that the child recalls earlier uses of the same word and connects them with the objects being referred to. The storing of such memories obviously begins in infancy, to accumulate a store or backlog to call on—so by not remembering his infancy Augustine does not remember such remembering, a thing that will puzzle him later on (T 10). But how can one not remember remembering? What is memory good for if it cannot even retain itself? The scale of this problem can be seen from the fact that Augustine, at the end of [14], just gives up trying to solve it.

8. Augustine's observation of his son and other infants made him marvel at the active, striving, acquiring energies of the child. Here was no tabula rasa to take an impression from the activity of others. His child grabs at the world and pulls large parts of it into himself. This picture is confirmed by a large modern body of ingenious experiments on the actions and responses of neonates, infants, toddlers—and even of the unborn, who now respond to experiments in the womb. I list just three books from the flourishing literature, each of which sums up other researchers' findings:

Steven Pinker, *The Language Instinct* (Harper/Perennial, 1994).
Ann B. Barnet and Richard J. Barnet, *The Youngest Minds* (Simon & Schuster, 1998).
Alison Gopnik, Andrew N. Meltzoff, and Patricia K. Kuhl, *The Scientist in the Crib* (William Morrow and Company, 1999).

What Augustine first notices about the infant's activities is its smile at its mother. Folklore cynicism has recently held that this is just a twisting of the mouth to ease the escape of gas, a kind of silent burp, but researchers find that it is one of the earliest manifestations of a sign language that precedes verbal expression and is an occasion for it—as Augustine will assert

([13]; *Teacher* [36]). Augustine no doubt recalled his favorite secular author's wonderful line, *Incipe, parve puer, risu cognoscere matrem* (Virgil, *Eclogues* 4.60), where the smile itself seems to have a cognitive power. Gopnik et al. (28–29) demonstrate that evolution (Augustine would say God) has rigged this early transmission of meaning by giving the newborn's eyes a focus of one foot—just the distance to the face of a nursing mother. The Barnets (p. 45) sum up further research on the encounter:

> Each mother-and-infant pair interacts in its own subtly different way, but the choreography is essentially the same: the meeting of eyes, the movements toward each other, the facial expressions and postures of the head and body changing ever so slightly to mirror the other. Child psychiatrists sometimes call this delicate and lovely expressiveness "attunement."

Augustine will describe the large attunements that made possible his easy acquisition of language as a child: "surrounded by nurses who coaxed, adults who laughed, and others fond of playing with a child" [23].

It is only within this primal communications system that the infant's anger at not getting the response he wants is explicable. He already knows that a response is possible, and resents it when the smiling mother does not pick him up, expose her nipple, or rock him when he wants it. Personal anger focuses as early as does the recognition of other persons. Gopnik et al. (p. 24) sum up their findings:

The new research in developmental psychology tells us that quite literally from the moment we first see other people, we see them as people. To be a person is to have a mind as well as a body, an inside as well as an outside. To see someone as a person is to see a face, not a mask; a "thou," not an "it." We arrive in the world with a set of profound assumptions about how other people are like us and how we are like other people.

Augustine knew that from his own "experiments"—by watching Godsend, his son.

9.   Augustine worries again the problem of how he came to exist without knowing he existed, in a sequence lost to him but obviously taking place in the timely unfolding of God's timeless rationale. Then, in a playful recasting of the child's smiling encounter *(ridere)* with the mother, he wonders if God smiles in gentle mockery *(inrides)* at his thrashing about for a meaning that is beyond him. The child's *aporia* is repeated in Augustine's testimony to his present incomprehension.

10.   The diminutive *mulierculae* ("little women") is dismissive, not of women as such, but of the weight of their evidence, since Augustine is stressing how slender are his proofs of anything about his infancy. Elsewhere, describing things we cannot know by direct evidence, he writes that we have nothing but faith in others' reports about the identity of our parents (*The Pragmatism of Belief* 26): "There is no way to reason our way to this. We have to take the mother's word for who the father is,

yet we cannot take the mother's own word—but that of mid-wives or nurses or servants—for who the mother is, since the mother herself can be deceived if the wet nurse gives her a different child after spiriting hers away."

The same kind of dismissiveness for a specific reason can be found in the only other use of *mulierculae* in *The Testimony* (6.24), where Augustine's earnest young Neoplatonist friends were prevented from forming an ascetic philosophical community because some had already established domestic arrangements with *mulierculae*—which has the force, here, of "homebodies." This, too, refers not to the inferiority of women as such (though Augustine, like most of his contemporaries, believed they were inferior), but to their lack of a philosophical turn. Monnica, to Augustine's surprise, showed a philosophical gift when she was finally admitted to the conversations of his circle at Cassiciacum.

11. In describing infant tantrums, Augustine dwells especially on one scene, which becomes for him almost as much the model of motiveless malignity as his theft of the pears would be in Book Two. The scene is one he clearly witnessed, and it depends on the African practice of using wet nurses. He has already told us [7] that he was suckled by his mother (at first) and by nurses—always used in the plural. He must have followed the same practice with his own son and seen him, or one of his peers, as they suckled at one of the wet nurse's nipples, push an infant away from her other nipple (this is the force of the word *con*-lactoneum, *fellow*-suckling). This was not done

out of hunger—the angry child was being fed, and Augustine told us in [7] that God supplies milk to fit the need. The baby could not be realizing that his nipple might run out if the other one were suckled. Augustine emphasizes that this is a real event: "With my own eyes I was a present witness [*Vidi ego et expertus sum*] of a tiny thing's fierce competitiveness."

The details are vivid and specific: "Though he could not speak, he made himself clear by his sudden pallor and the sour contortion of his features." The adjective *amaro* (sour) means he is screwing up his face as at the taste of something bitter. Compare the way Cain's "face is contorted" by envy of his brother Abel at Genesis 4.6, referred to by Augustine as the expression of envy (T 4.9). The infant at the nipple is not quite Cain slaying Abel, but he is trying in his feeble way to do something similar, "to deprive another of the one food it depends on." As with the case of the pears, Augustine is not looking at what later moralists would call "parvity of matter," but at the intent. The infant is clearly trying to harm another infant for no good reason—as the infant tries to harm adults when he does not get his way, "to hurt (if he could) those who dare disobey his own self-harming ukase."

The modern reader will, of course, think Augustine is too hard on infants, demonstrating his general pessimism and his specific preoccupation with "original sin." But we are thinking mainly in terms of morals, while his concern might more properly be called metaphysical. He is not trying to indict the child but to ponder the origin of evil. He has said, and he will repeat, that everything was good about the way he was brought into being. God himself formed him, framed the marvelous circuitry of his perceptive apparatus [12], providentially supplied the very milk in his nurses' breasts [7]—yet here is something not-good on the scene. Excusable perhaps, given that it is just an infant acting. But the behavior in itself is not good, as Augustine proves by showing that it would be condemned if indulged by those without extenuating youth. He is not concerned with blaming the child but with explaining how bad behavior can occur in a good universe. The child's case puts the mystery in its starkest terms, as Graham Greene realized in his tales of perverse children. G. K. Chesterton argued in the same way when he said that original sin becomes easier to understand at the moment when, on a long summer's afternoon, bored children begin to torture the cat.

Evil, for Augustine, is a lack, a gap in the good universe caused not by its creator but by a free will that can choose the lesser good in defiance of the higher; opening up, as it were, a crevice between one good and another, affording a glimpse into the abyss of the non-good, the anti-being. This makes the gears slip, causes a disconnect or slippage between what should be and what is. Only the human will can do this, and *Mos* (Custom), the solidarity of the willing human community, has made it occur as a general phenomenon after Adam's fall. That is what is happening in the nursery as Augustine watches.

For the modern reader, who believes in evolution, the baby's strivings are part of the general competitive struggle to survive, one that will be refined with success, moving from brute struggling to more intellectual efforts at mastery. Progress is from the lower to the higher. But Augustine believed that all creation is from God and was good in itself to begin with. Non-good behavior could only come about by defection from an original *bonum*, a motion from the higher to the lower—until God should check the downward spiral by his redemptive mission in Jesus. Accepting his own unremembered but undoubted sin as an infant, Augustine expresses the need for such redemption from the general perversity of fallen human beings. That perversity is best established if it can be found in even the most "innocent" condition of infancy. If universally good behavior is not found there, where can it be found? "Nowhere outside Christ" is Augustine's proclamation in his prayer.

12. Augustine re-emphasizes that the child lives in creation where everything God made is good, beginning with himself. His own body is a miracle, and Augustine singles out three aspects of it reflective of the Trinity that created it—his sensory system, his physical organization, and a superintending unity. First, "how you articulate *(instruxisti)* its sensory apparatus." *Instruo* was said of arranging complex items like battle formations. The wonder of sensation was especially impressive to Augustine, since he thought external pressures on the body were not the source of sensation. He held that the inferior cannot determine the superior, that the body cannot dictate to the soul. He compared the external world's action to knocking on the portals of the senses, which the soul must open to emerge and seize the sensation. The soul itself acts, apprehending sights, sounds, smells, et cetera. The soul acts instantaneously,

shooting out (e.g.) its rays to distant visibles ("Open your eye and you are there," *Sermon* 277.10). The soul is entirely present in its every act of sensations ("entire in each"), and it creates the internal image of external things by a reflection of God's creative power (*The Trinity* 16.2).

So powerful is the soul's active power of imaging things, its ability to mold an inner reality, that Augustine wondered at this creativity even in sinful misuses of it (*Trinity* 11.2.7): "I recall hearing from a man that he could ordinarily hold in thought such a solid and, as it were, tangible image of a woman's body that he felt as if he were in intercourse with her, to the point of ejaculation, so strong is the power of the soul's imaging over the body—it can shift the body around, the way the body shifts the hanging of a cloak by its motions, making the cloak conform to its contours." However man misuses this mental control of the body through the instruments of the senses, it remains a miraculous dispensation for Augustine. We shall hear in the next paragraph how a baby "grabs" *(prendere)* the sound of a word, a perfect instance of the *active* power of sensation that Augustine admired.

In a second endowment of the child, God "fits limb to limb" (*compingere*, from *pangere*, means to glue things into each other), giving beauty to its form. The symmetry and beauty of the human body was a prime example for Augustine of "number," the attribute of the Second Person of the Trinity. Here "number" means the harmonious relationship of part to part, making the body "numerous" *(numerosum)*, while especially beautiful bodies are *numerosiora* (*Music* 6.4.7). Indeed, Augustine says that the beauty of the body transcends even its adaptation to the requirements of survival (*Trinity* 22.24):

> Entirely apart from the body's operational equipment, the coherence of all its parts is so proportionate *(numerosa)*, and their responsiveness to each other is so beautiful, that one cannot say whether form or function ranked first in the composition of it. . . . But since no component (at least of those visible enough to be judged unerringly) is so devoted to useful function as to exclude beauty, and some have beauty without function, I think it is easy to see that splendor was preferred to utility. The need for utility will pass, the time will come when we shall take delight simply in each other's beauty, with no taint of lust—to the glory of the Creator, as the Psalmist says [104.1]: 'You clothed us in beauty as a testimony *(confessionem)* to you.'

This "testimony" of beauty shows how one-sided are old notions of *The Testimony* as mainly concerned with sin. Throughout the book, Augustine is testifying as well to God's gifts, wonders, and grace.

The third endowment of the baby is a coordinating unity in all its different components' actions, the binding together in love that is a prerogative of the Third Person of the Trinity. The organic oneness of any living thing made Augustine marvel even at the lower animals (*True Religion* 77):

> I could descant in all candor on the glories of the worm, when I look at its iridescence, its perfect corporeal rotundity, its interaction of end with middle, middle with end, each contributing

to a thrust toward oneness in this lowest of things, so that there is no part that does not answer to another part harmoniously. And what of the principle of life effervescing its melodious order through this body?—its rhythmic activation of the whole, its quest for that which serves its life, its triumph over or revulsion from what threatens it, its reference of all things to a normative center of self-preservation, bearing witness more striking than the body's to the creative unity that upholds all things in nature?

One interesting thing about this passage is the way it seems to grant some validity to the evolutionary struggle ("its triumph over or revulsion from what threatens it")—a hint conveyed elsewhere as well (*Order in the Universe* 1.25). But he could justify any person's deliberately harming another—who, is, after all, the image of the Trinity—only in exercises of individual or corporate self-defense.

Augustine moves from the traces of the trinity to the Trinity itself when he celebrates the oneness, and beauty, and law that emanate their energies throughout creation. Only God can "from your oneness, give each thing its degree [*modus*] of being; from your beauty give it shapeliness [*forma*]; from your law [*lex*] give it its rank in creation." This triad is a correlative of the one in Wisdom 11.21 [1]. *Modus* is like *mensura* in delimiting the extent of existence in its various manifestation. *Forma* is like *numerus*, the melodic principle of unity. And *lex* is like *pondus*, the compulsion that assigns each thing its ordered place.

III. Childhood (Speaking)

13. Since speech distinguishes childhood from pre-verbal (and pre-remembering) infancy, this first paragraph on Augustine's childhood deals directly with the subject of speech, and tells us how Augustine taught himself to talk. Taught *himself*—that is the most surprising assertion of the whole paragraph. Unfortunately, it is the one thing in the paragraph that Wittgenstein, in his 1934 notes of *The Brown Book* (Blackwell, 1972, p. 77), ignores or denies: "Augustine, in describing his learning of language, says that he *was taught* to speak by learning the names of things" [emphasis added]. He goes on to say that Augustine just relates words to physical objects, not to the relationships and structures that make up language, nor to abstractions or actions: "It is clear that whoever says this has in mind the way in which a child learns such words as 'man,' 'sugar,' 'table,' etc. He does not primarily think of such words as 'today,' 'not,' 'but,' 'perhaps.' " In his better-known passage, opening the *Philosophical Investigations* (Anscombe translation, Blackwell, 1968, p. 2): "Augustine does not speak of there being any difference between kinds of words. If you describe the learning of language in this way you are, I believe, thinking primarily of nouns like 'table,' 'chair,' 'bread,' and of people's names, and only secondarily of the names of certain actions

and properties." This, Wittgenstein says, is not so much teaching as "training," as one does dogs, by pointing to things and making a sound ("ostension").

But if Wittgenstein had bothered to look at *The Teacher*, he could not have said that Augustine "does not speak of there being any difference between kinds of words." Augustine did not restrict himself to words like "table," but asked his son to give the meaning of words exactly like those Wittgenstein said he excluded. The modern philosopher wonders what Augustine would make of "not" and "but." Augustine asked Godsend to explain "nothing" and "from" at *The Teacher* 3–4, and "if" at (9), as well as to distinguish "because" from "if" at (16). He clearly saw the need to go beyond "ostensive" language (pointing to a table)—and this in a dialogue that precedes *The Testimony* and that he says at the end of his life he still agrees with.

Yet one does not have to appeal to *The Teacher* to see that Wittgenstein is distorting what is in Book One of *The Testimony*. First, look at what is said of the process: "These words, used in their right way in different grammatical settings [*variis sententiis locis suis posita*], and recurring over time, I steadily accumulated . . ." To measure the full force of that phrase, we must remember that Latin is an inflected language. Augustine would not have learned *this* word means *that* thing by recognizing a single word, say *tabula* for "table." He would, according to the use of the word in its right place in various sentences, have heard *tabulae, tabulam, tabula, tabulae, tabularum, tabulis,* and *tabulas.* Not only that, if he were to understand them in their various sentences, he would have to grasp the difference between *tabulae* as genitive singular or nominative plural or vocative plural, and the difference between *tabula* as nominative and as ablative, the difference between *tabulis* as dative and as ablative, and so on. And that was just beginning of the connections to be learned along with the words. Pronouns have several roots (*ego* but *mihi*) as well as all those cases. Verbs had even more forms than nouns, including tenses. It seems impossible that these could be learned one by one according to external rules—and it *is* impossible. Augustine, like modern experimenters, denies that they are learned. What the words refer to (the physical table) is pointed out, but the words act according to a system that is not learned but intuited. Wittgenstein said Augustine described the learning of inert single words outside a language system, but Augustine could not have thought in those terms. The Latin words did not exist without their inflections, and the inflections put them inescapably inside a system. Augustine could not store them up and use them outside that system.

In fact, experiments on children show that they do learn words *in their functions,* not apart from them. Given sentences calling for word formations they have not heard and cannot be parroting, children "invent" logical extensions of the forms they have heard (Pinker, p. 276). They have an inbuilt system of their own. The external system is not imported into them; it stimulates and confirms the internal system (while giving some arbitrary material like the names of things to be processed in the system). This is what Chomsky calls a "generative grammar," one developed from within, not imposed from without.

America's greatest classical scholar, Basil Gildersleeve, described something similar when he said that the archaic Greeks knew grammar before the rules of grammar were formulated. They had no grammatical mistakes, just "mispronunciations." The grammatical way of saying things was more *seen* (or heard) than taught. Although we do not have a heavily inflected grammar like Latin, it has been proved that children learn the right way of identifying words when they are spoken in all kinds of different accents and in odd constructions. They recognize them *because* of their connectedness with other words, not despite it.

Each child, according to the Chomskian linguist Steven Pinker, invents its own language, even though it turns out to be everybody else's language too. There is a language system that goes with being human, just as two arms and two legs do. That is the situation we have evolved to. The system can be damaged or developed poorly—or even be missing from the outset—just as arms and legs can. But we no more introject language into the child than we can stick arms or legs on it. They are already there: "The crux of the argument is that complex language is universal because children actually reinvent it, generation after generation—not because they are taught, not because they are generally smart, not because it is useful to them, but because they just can't help it" (Pinker, p. 32).

I said above that there were two things in Book One that should have prevented Wittgenstein from reaching his simplistic view of Augustine's position. The first was the linguistic *embeddedness* of the words Augustine was learning. The second is the semantic system that was stimulating and confirming the innate verbal system—that other language, "body language." This is not just a matter of pointing with one's finger. There is an elaborate enacting process that goes on when people communicate, and especially when they communicate with children. Augustine describes it this way: "facial expressions, glances, or miming actions . . . conveying an intention to get or retain, repel or evade something." This goes far beyond "ostension" of a table. Augustine limns in his words a vast emotional repertoire for indicating not just things but attitudes, actions, desires, judgments, or doubts. I translate as "miming actions" the words "enactment of other body parts [then the face]" because at *The Teacher* 6 he describes actors and ballet dancers who can tell whole stories without using words. In *Christian Culture* (2.3.4) he describes languages that can do without words: "We can, by moves of the head, convey what we want to the eyes alone. Certain gestures of the hand are full of significance, and actors can with their whole body make others understand them, in a conversation of the eyes, while soldiers manipulate flags and battle standards to issue orders from their generals. All of these are the equivalent of an eye language [*verba visibilia*]."

Nor is body language entirely divorced from words. Modern experimenters show how attuned are children to tone of voice, inflection, facial frowns and smiles, and sound patterns of their native tongue—all of these going along with the contents of the word as a kind of *music* of meaning. They even acquire a feel for this music, from their mother's voice, within the womb.

Since this musical language *is* a language, it is good for stimulating or confirming the language system already in the child. To read this language takes an innate skill like that which the verbal system cues.

Augustine shows that, despite all the skill of the mime-dancer, the physical demonstrations are not perspicuous in themselves. The example he uses in *The Teacher* (6) is the person who gets up and walks when asked what the word "walking" means. The demonstration is not sufficient in itself. One might take it to mean that walking is hurrying or lingering, or going far. In fact, unless one *keeps* walking to and over the horizon, it might even mean *stopping* when the walking ends. But this objection applies equally to simple "ostensive" identification of a word as well as demonstration of an act, as Pinker (p. 153) illustrates, using an example from the logician E.V.O. Quine:

> A rabbit scurries by, and a native shouts, "Gavagai!" What does *gavagai* mean? Logically speaking, it needn't be "rabbit." It could refer to that particular mammal, or any member of that species of rabbit (say, *oryctolagus cuniculus*), or any member of that variety of species (say, chinchilla rabbit). It could mean scurrying rabbit, scurrying thing, rabbit plus the ground it scurries upon, or scurrying in general. It could mean footprint-maker, or habitat for rabbit-fleas. It could mean the top half of a rabbit, or rabbit-meat-on-the-hoof, or possessor of at least one rabbit's foot. It could mean anything that is either a rabbit or a Buick. It could mean collection of undetached rabbit parts, or

"Lo! Rabbithood again!" or "It rabbiteth," analogous to "It raineth."

Then how do people take the right meaning out of such inherently ambiguous signaling? By a grasp of the intention of the speaker that reads whole systems as presciently as the internal language system reads words in their relationships. The Barnets (p. 40) put it this way:

> Our ability to communicate also depends on our using and understanding, in differing ways in various cultures and circumstances, the raised eyebrow, the pregnant pause, the shrugged shoulder, the inclined head, the raised hand. We depend upon the concept of symbolic utterance, and on our ability to make use of symbolic utterances, to connect the idea in our heads with the object out there, or to an action, an intention, or a stream of ideas and feelings.

Augustine realized [23] that the ease with which he learned his first language, Latin, came in part from "nurses who coaxed, adults who laughed, and others fond of playing with a child." He generalized this in his pedagogy, saying that one learns best in an atmosphere of love. In *First Instruction* 17 he advises those teaching catechumens to "put ourselves in their affectionate brother's place, or their mother's or father's ... The more, by the bond of love, we enter into each other's mind, the more even old things become new for us again." And in *Christian Culture* (Preface 12): "Though love unites us in close ties, it would have no channel for souls to flow into each other and mingle unless each were learning from the other." He remembered his companionship with a young Manichaean circle as almost replicating the sign system of the nursery: "Reciprocated love uses such semaphorings—a smile, a glance, a thousand winning acts—to fuse separate sparks into a single glow, no longer many souls, but one" (T 4.17).

But after making a broad argument on the ability of body language to convey meaning, Augustine says that the response to these signals, like that to language in general, is a matter of confirming the interior system that tests and establishes the child's innate language sense. What Chomsky calls an innate language-creating capacity, and Gopnik et al. call a gift perfected by evolution, Augustine calls the inner light given by God to each person coming into the world. In fact, Jerry A. Fodor says that Wittgenstein stumbled on a truth in what he thought of as a criticism of Augustine. Here is *Philosophical Investigations* (pp. 15–16): "Augustine describes the learning of human language as if the child came into a strange country and did not understand the language of the country; that is, as if it already had a language, only not this one. Or again: as if the child could already *think*, only not speak. And 'think' would here mean something like 'talk to itself.' " But Chomsky and others say that the child does have its own internal language for talking to itself (what Pinker calls "mentalese"). Fodor concludes (*The Language of Thought*, Crowell, 1975, p. 64):

So one cannot learn a language unless one has a language. In particular, one cannot learn a first language unless one already has a system capable of representing the predicates in that language *and their extension.* And, on pain of circularity, that system cannot be the language being learned. . . . Wittgenstein apparently takes it that such a view [as Augustine's] is transparently absurd. But the argument that I just sketched suggests, on the contrary, that Augustine was precisely and demonstrably right, and that seeing that he was is prerequisite to any serious attempts to understand how first languages are learned [emphasis in the original].

Language as innate is an evolved faculty for most modern observers (though Chomsky cannot imagine how a process of natural selection could account for it—see his *The Architecture of Language,* pp. 49–50). For Augustine it was part of the "illumination" that God grants each individual, what the Gospel of John (1.9) calls "the light enlightening every man who comes into the world." For Augustine, the mind can no more see truth without this light than the eye can see objects without an external physical light. He applied to the process what his version of Psalm 35.10 said: "By your light we shall see light." In order to think at all, he argued, the mind must generate an internal *verbum,* a mental word, by a process that dimly echoes the eternal generation of the *Verbum* by God the Father (*The Trinity,* 15.20). This mental language resembles (in result, not cause) what Pinker calls the mental language that precedes spoken language in babies. And all understanding of truth takes place through the inner Illumination that makes the divine *Verbum* stand warrant for each of our tested and truthful *verba.*

That is why Augustine says that, when it comes to *understanding* any proposition (his definition of knowledge, *scientia*), there can be no external teacher, just the inner one—the point of his dialogue with his son: "You have only one Teacher . . . for you have only one Father in heaven" (Matthew 23.8–9).

According to *The Teacher*, when the child pulls into its mind the conventional (arbitrary) words that others are using for external things, he is acquiring the counters by which he can communicate with others, who have their own "mental language" but need external signals of it. The real learning goes on in that mental language, which comes not from the external world but from God. The external teacher can give information about the arbitrary sign system, or draw attention to a subject—the parallel is with external objects "knocking at the door" for sensation to let it in. Some have compared this external teacher in Augustine to Socrates' conception of himself as an intellectual midwife (Plato, *Theaetetus* 149). But it is important to note the differences between Plato and Augustine on this point. In *Theaetetus*, an important role is that of the maieutic attendant, "Doctor" Socrates. Augustine, by contrast, is a self-deliverer of his thought, divinely pushed from within, not pulled from without: "From my own heart's need I went into labor to deliver . . ."**[23]**. Nor is the knowledge delivered by the child a result of some Platonic memory *(anamnesis)* from a former existence. It comes from God's illumination of the mind *at the moment.* There are many secular objections that can be made to this doctrine, but Wittgenstein's claim that it involves a simplistic view of language is entirely outside the realm being discussed. That is why it is important to read this section of *The Testimony* in conjunction with *The Teacher*.

14. From this paragraph on, Book One finds the child Augustine caught between two groups of adults. One is made up of his teachers, who are driving him on a course of worldly ambition. They want him to be skilled in the rhetorical use of language, but they do not use language to persuade him of the wisdom of their course. They beat him, confessing the weakness of their own persuasive rhetoric. The other group is made up of those who believe in God, and in prayer to him. This refers clearly to the church his mother took him to. Membership in an African church of the time involved very close ties of community, guarded by strict standards of conduct, and by excommunication if those were broken. Among other things, there was a siege mentality caused by competition with the schismatic Donatist churches paired off with Catholic ones. This is the time when Augustine acquired his affection for the very name of Christ (T 4.8), one he missed in later engagements with pagan philosophy and Jewish Scripture (though not with Manichaeism, which honored Christ).

15. Augustine is confused by the way his parents stand between the two groups of adults in his life, the church and his teachers, laughing when he prays to the martyrs (specially honored in Africa after the persecutions there) and supporting the school discipline. The confusion this caused in him may account for the way the paragraph opens with one of the rare

clumsy sentences of *The Testimony*. One may suspect cor-
ruption of the text, since it makes no sense as it stands. It is a
comparison, of martyrs *so (itu)* disposed *as (quemadmodum)*
parents. But (in the best manuscripts) it asks if martyrs so *love*
those who fear pain as parents *laugh at* children who fear pain.
The *comparanda* do not conform to each other, and the long
parenthesis (martyrs facing all pains, others fearing them) are
semi-humorous exaggerations of Augustine's own childish
fears of being beaten. The point should be that martyrs might
have a *right* to laugh at the fearful, but the parents, who are not
such heroes in facing pain, do not. That meaning is achieved if
we follow the reading of one manuscript, *deridens,* for *diligens.*
The last word could have been imported by a confused scribe
who remembered that Augustine had just said that his parents
"were not wishing me ill." The sense then is: would even heroic
bearers of pain think little of the less heroic, as my parents
thought of me? The next sentence shows that the hyperbolic
parenthesis on suffering is what was mainly on Augustine's
mind: *I* was not less afraid than those who trembled at mar-
tyrdom. This sentence should determine what the *comparanda* are. The triple play on *minus* in the next sentence shows
that there is a note of self-satire, of hyperbolic description, running through both sentences.

Augustine will not let his teachers off the hook. Though he
admits he had no right to evade his studies, since he did not do
it for any higher purpose (just to indulge his love of games), he
turns around and says that the teachers were playing more sin-
ister games. He is angry that they made him fear them so. It

was probably the contrast between these terror merchants and the more humane pagan he met in Madauros, Maximus, that first lured Augustine into his adolescent paganism (*Letters* 16, 17). In that case, he resents the fact that the flagellant tutors frightened him away from the faith.

17.   The clash between adults over Augustine's future career reached a climax when his lung problems threatened his life. (He would always have some weakness of the lungs, which he later used as an excuse to escape from his court position in Milan.) The equivocation of his parents also reaches a climax. Augustine himself, not his mother, initiates the request for baptism—begs it, not only from his own mother but from "mother church" (another sign of the degree to which he was integrated into the Catholic community's liturgical life as a child). Though his mother anxiously complies while the illness persists, she relapses into the worldly judgment of others as soon as it passes. This is one of several places where he indicates that Monnica was not yet the model of piety that would later be made of her (O 2.308). At T 1.8, for instance, he says that, while living with him in Carthage, she was only in the "outskirts" of God's favor. His famous tribute to her at T 9.17–37 is a form of funeral tribute, in which, as Samuel Johnson reminds us, one does not speak on oath.

18.   It is not surprising that Augustine would take the position as bishop that he was urging on his own congregation— that Christians should be baptized as children and live all their

lives in the church. We would find it hard to regret that he had the great experience of living with a woman he loved and raising a child close to his heart. But one of the things he reproached himself with was the way he drew his loving partner away from the practice of her own faith for so many years. He would never admit that sin should be indulged for the good that might come of it.

IV. Schooling

23. The image of words' internal conception and delivery into the ears of others, already discussed, is spelled out here. It was an image he explored ever more thoroughly, since it showed to Augustine how the structure of the Trinity is reflected in human generation of a *verbum mentis* that is then "born" into the external world. This was not only a type of the Trinity, but of the Incarnation, since God's Word takes on flesh in order to reach humans who will believe in it. As Augustine will put in *The Trinity* 9.12–13:

> We *conceive* a true knowledge of things as an enunciation to ourselves, begetting it as an inner word which does not leave us when it is delivered by *birth* [to others]. Rather, when we speak to others, we join to that inner word either our voice or some other material sign, as a kind of physical [incarnated] report of what remains in the mind of the speaker even as it conveys something similar to the mind of the hearer. . . . Now this word is conceived out of love—love for creatures or for their creator, for changeable beings or changeless truth. . . . But it is born when, out of pondering it, we act [or speak] either sinfully or virtuously. In this way a union between begetting mind and begotten word is effected by love, which makes a third member in this embrace of things at one with each other but also distinct.

V. Conforming to a Deforming Society

25. The ways of human Society *(Mos)* play the same role, at the public level, that *Consuetudo* (Habit) does at the private level—see T 8.10, where he describes habit as the chain one forges around oneself. The difficulty of breaking habits is treated in Augustine's *Sermon* 307.5, where he describes how hard it was for him to discontinue his swearing of oaths (against the scriptural prohibition at Matthew 5.33–37). *Mos* is the communal habit that pressures one to internalize it as *consuetudo*. In **[26]**, for instance, the *Mos* that condones the use of Jove's rape as a respected model leads to the *consuetudo* of indulged lust.

26. For us, the offense of the Terentian passage (if any) would be its sexual naughtiness. But we are not tempted to believe in Jove. Augustine's contemporaries still were. Many then remembered the Emperor Julian's revival of the pagan system in the second half of the century that was ending as Augustine wrote, and modern scholars have shown how thin a veneer was Constantinian Christianity over a world still largely pagan What bothered Augustine in the play was less its low morals than its delusive religion.

27.　In the fond description of his heart being trellised up around the supporting study of Scripture, Augustine regrets that he was not given the kind of mental formation he outlines and advocates in *Christian Culture* (as Peter Brown calls *De Doctrina Christiana*).

28.　The idea of being far off from God often triggers in Augustine a reminiscence of the prodigal son's going to a "far country." This first reference to the parable of the younger son is followed by other references in *The Testimony*, direct or indirect—so much so that Georg Nicolaus Knauer argued that the entire book is structured around the parable ("Peregrinatio Animae," *Hermes* 85, 1957, pp. 216–46). But this is just one of the many "strayings" that Augustine took from scriptural imagery of paths (see Introduction: The Book's Imagery). What is important in this paragraph is the equation of the son's return to his father with the return of the soul to the One in Plotinus.

30.　This paragraph summarizes the sins of Augustine's boyhood, moving backward in time from the point his narrative has reached. He begins with his most recently acquired faults, the same snobbishness about committing solecisms that he imbibed from his teachers, despite the defiance he showed them in lying to escape their classes—which was done, not from any high principle, but to indulge in plays and games that undermine morals. Going even further back into his boyhood, he recalls how he stole food from his parents' house to bribe playmates into letting him play with them. Then he cheated those who admitted him into their circle, while hypocritically attacking them for doing the same thing. He was, without knowing it, pre-enacting all the follies and faults that make up secular life, doing for game prizes what adults do for gold. The innocence of children is a myth.

The emphasis on deception in this summary is typical of a man who came to prize truthfulness as the essential virtue for one dealing with a God who is Truth. He *lied* to pedagogue and tutor, to mother and father, when he evaded class or stole food. He lied in two ways with his playfellows, while cheating and while objecting to cheats. As he says, the role models proposed for him were hardly ones to show him how wrong this was. The art of rhetoric, as he was instructed in it, was a way of coloring or distorting truth for advantage. His masters preferred a lie, or any other wrong, to an embarrassing slip in grammar or pronunciation.

31. Yet the book cannot end, self-centeredly, on what was wrong (i.e., what was his) in Augustine's boyhood. He was, after all, an image of the Trinity. "I existed [*modus*], I experienced sensation [*numerus*], I preserved myself—by an echo of your mysterious oneness [*pondus*]." The book then ends in a swirl of triads: *joy-glory-truth*, played against *pain-dejection-error*, leading to *delight-pride-trust*.

PART IV

Appendix: *The Teacher*

Introduction

This dialogue of Augustine with his sixteen-year-old son Godsend was composed in 389–390 C.E., when the two had returned to Africa after their baptism in Milan. With a small group of friends gathered in his native city of Thagaste, Augustine intended to create a library of Christian knowledge, an encyclopedic project begun in Milan and carried forward in a connected series of dialogues on different topics. The whole project was abandoned when Augustine was compelled to accept priesthood in 391 at Hippo, where his pastoral duties supervened. One reason for Augustine's removal to Hippo may have been the death of his son soon after this dialogue with him was completed. There was no reason for Augustine to superintend the family property now that there would be no heir of his to use it. In fact, family memories with his brother and sister and their children might have been sad in these circumstances. One reason for his returning to Thagaste in the first place might have been to keep his son near his mother, if (as I have argued elsewhere) Thagaste was her hometown, to which she had returned.

Augustine's practice in these early dialogues was to carry on a real discussion, taken down by stenographers, and then to polish the resulting text. He assures us (T 9.14) that all the re-

sponses *(sensa)* made by Godsend in this published work were
actually voiced by him in the original conversation. Given
Augustine's scrupulous standard of truthfulness, we can assume that he edited Godsend's words very lightly, preserving
their point. The result is a wonderful record of the two men's
relationship—one of deep mutual respect that did not preclude
a joshing familiarity. Godsend does not hesitate to tease his father, cleverly saying that he will answer Augustine's questions
without using words when the questions are asked without
words (5). When Augustine suggests that the word *nothing*
might be meaningless, Godsend says (3) that only a fool would
use a meaningless word—so why was Augustine using it?
The son wonders (15) whether the father can come up with a
master rhetorician to answer their questions—knowing that
Augustine is supposed to be the master rhetorician. After Augustine posits a whiz of an intellect to cope with one problem,
Godsend says he could as easily posit a whiz to solve another
problem they had found unsolvable (32). When the father asks
what his son thought of his "entire" speech, Godsend admits
that it *was* rather long—in fact, *perpetua* (46). A professor of
philosophy tells me that this dialogue is a welcome break from
Plato's, where Socrates manipulated intellectual patsies. Two
real minds are shown at work in *The Teacher*.

The warmth of the dialogue does not come across in most
translations of it, for two reasons—of style and of method. In
style, the dialogue imitates those of Cicero, where the inflected
Latin leads, even in informal exchanges, to circumlocution, a
kind of "structurey" throat-clearing, and delay of the emphatic

matter to the end of the sentence. This is not so much a problem in *The Testimony*, where the psalm-couplet style led to parataxis instead of periodicity. But normal Latin uses transitions like *quae cum ita sint*, "if this should be [subjunctive] how things are," where we would use, according to context, pithier conjunctions. Thus when Augustine asks Godsend at the beginning of *The Teacher*, "Why do we talk to each other," the answer in Latin is: *Quantum quidem mihi nunc occurrit, aut docere aut discere*—literally, "Insofar as comes to me at the moment, either to teach or to learn." The punchy *docere . . . discere* is saved for the emphatic spot, after some periphrastic groping. The natural way to say this in English, which favors emphasis at the outset, is: "To teach or be taught—that's my hunch." This is not departing from what was said, it *is* what was said—but as it would be said in English. So in this translation I try to avoid the structurey transitions and pleonasms, informal in the original, that just sound artificial in our idiom.

The *method* that makes this dialogue sound more stilted than natural is what Augustine himself calls its "verbal jousting" technique (31). The preliminary arguments are all limbering-up exercises, in which conclusions are reached, or exceptions allowed, that are canceled later, but not necessarily explicitly. As M. F. Burnyeat writes, in the best commentary on the dialogue: "This bewildering sequence of about-turns shows that Augustine, like Plato often (and Wittgenstein), is determined not to tell us how to read his writings."[1] Yet Augustine explained his method in a work he was completing as he conducted the dialogue with his son, the *Music*. He moves from the outer to the inner, from the physical to the spiritual, devoting the first five books to metrics in song and verse before moving in the last book to the music of the spheres and the beauty of Number in the mind. He explains the transition in 6.1, where he hopes "the reader will understand that this lowly road is not of lowly value—it is, in fact, the one I have trudged along with the weak (being no athlete myself), rather than commit unfledged wings at once to thin air."

In *The Teacher*, Augustine first deals with the sign system of words considered in their taxonomic and external aspect, before moving to the mind's own inner language, by which it tests what it apprehends by the senses. The argument is one long paradox:

> Nothing can be taught but by signs.
> *But:* Signs cannot teach.
> *So:* Nothing can be taught.

Augustine is not denying that we get information from others, but this process is not understanding *(scientia)*, it is trust *(fides)* in the "say-so" of another. It is the difference between taking a teacher's word for it on the solution of a geometry problem and "seeing" it oneself. Thus all our historical knowledge, or knowledge of others' states of mind, is based on acts of faith. He does not deny—how could he?—the importance, even the necessity of faith. In his books *The Pragmatism of Belief (De Utilitate Credendi)* and *Various Subjects (De Diversis Questionaibus,* Number 30), he makes the distinction between necessary means one uses *(uti)* for an end, and the fulfillment *(frui)* of things accepted for their own sake. So faith is a means on this earth to reach the fulfilling vision of God in heaven. (Saint Paul says faith and hope are the means, love the end, at 1 Corinthians 13.13).

Understanding *(scientia)* is a different matter. No one can understand for us. We do that by our innate mental powers, which operate in the light of God's truth. Others can "post a sign" *(admonere)* for us to exercise our understanding on, but—as Burnyeat puts it—this is just "providing an occasion" for our inner powers to operate. Thus when Augustine uses, provisionally, the example of a bird catcher teaching by showing how he operates, we are meant to see the narrowness of the term "teach" in this sense:

> If showing or teaching requires no more than deliberately so acting or arranging things that other people may, if they wish, learn for themselves, then nothing is easier and the bird catcher is a perfectly good teacher. What Augustine is denying when he reaches his conclusion [that humans do not teach each other] is that anyone can do what telling is supposed to do, namely, transmit knowledge to another mind. On that commonsense understanding of "teaching," the bird catcher does not teach.[2]

Burnyeat argues that Augustine has, on his own, arrived at Plato's distinction between "true judgment" and *episteme,* calling them "trust" and *scientia. Scientia,* like *episteme,* must be firsthand knowledge, personal, justified by one's own reason:

It is eloquent testimony both to Augustine's philosophical acumen and to the coherence of the Platonic epistemology that Augustine should have been able to reconstruct it, on the basis of a quite new set of arguments, so much better than many who have actually read Plato's dialogues. Whatever is to be said about Adeodatus, of Augustine at least it is true that he learned it for himself, without being taught.[3]

Notes

1. M. F. Burnyeat, "Wittgenstein and Augustine *De Magistro*," Inaugural Address as president of the Aristotelian Society, *Proceedings* 1987, p. 14.
2. Ibid., p. 15.
3. Ibid., p. 22. Though some have compared Augustine's questioning of his son with Socrates' questioning of the slave in *Meno*, Burnyeat notes that Augustine "does not know what questions Socrates put to the slave . . . because he read about the *Meno* in Cicero [but not the *Meno* itself]."

The Teacher

1

Father: Why, in your view, do we talk to each other?

Son: To teach or be taught—that's my hunch.

F I am with you on the first, since we clearly talk in order to teach. But what makes you say we talk in order to be taught?

S Why do we ask questions if not to be taught?

F I suspect that even then we are trying to teach—don't you suppose we teach those we question what we want from them?

S That's true.

F Is it agreed, then, that we talk for no other reason than to teach?

S I don't quite follow that—after all, if talking is just saying words, I find that we do that when singing a song, and since we often sing when alone, with no one there to be taught, I don't see how we can be singing in order to teach.

F I believe there is a way of teaching, and not the least way, that is a recalling—as will come out in the very discussion we are having now. But if you do not yet agree that we are taught when we recall, or that we teach when we remind, I will not dispute this, but I advance the minimal point that two possible reasons for talking are to teach or to remind, either ourselves or others—which we do even when singing, won't you agree?

S Not really. It is not often I sing to remind myself. I do so to enjoy myself.

F I see what you are getting at, but haven't you noticed that the enjoyment of song comes from the windings of the tune, to which words can be supplied or from which they can be removed, marking the difference between singing and talking?[1] Tunes can be played on flutes and harps, and birds sing tunes, and we too can make music without words, which can be called tunes but not talk, right?

S Right.

2

F Do you concede, then, that talking has only two functions, for teaching or reminding?

S I might, if it did not occur to me that praying is a way of talking, and surely it is impossible for God to be taught, or to be reminded of anything by us.

F It is for this very reason (I'm sure you realize) that we are instructed to 'pray in our inmost chambers,' a term for our soul's deep recess—because when we ask what we most direly need, God is not waiting to be reminded or taught what that is. One who talks is varying conventional noises to signal the wants within him outward to others. But God is sought and prayed to precisely through our unexpressed interior wants, by a call within, in the temple whose consecration he desires—you have read, of course, the Apostle [Paul] saying, 'Do you not see that you are God's temple, and his Spirit makes his home in you?' Or, elsewhere, 'Christ is found in humanity's depths'? Or do you doubt the prophet's [David's] words, 'Talk inside your inmost self, and reform yourself in your bedchamber, where the offering to be made is a conduct reformed and a trust in God's mercy.' Where do you suppose the offering of right conduct could be made but in the temple of the soul, in the bedchamber of the affections—that is the temple of our offerings, the established place of prayer. That is why talking is not needed for praying—unless, of course, priests talk, to signal outward their interior message; not that God should hear, but that men should, who, when they hear, are jointly reminded of their dependence on God. Do you agree so far?

S Certainly.

F Aren't you bothered that the highest teacher of all, when he taught followers to pray, gave them specific words [to the Our Father]—was not this very clearly telling them that one must talk in order to pray?

S That is not confusing, since he did not teach the words but a reality behind the words, using words to refer us back to him, indicating to whom and how we should pray in the inmost chamber of the self—where, as you said, we do our praying.

F You get the point—I suppose you also realize that, if anyone says we talk inwardly to ourselves, by thinking of words but not saying them, this "talking" is nothing but remembering the things the words indicate. By our recurrence to them we bring to mind the realities of which they are the signs.

S I see that, and keep step with you.

3

F We agree, then, that words are signs?

S Of course.

F And can a sign be a sign without something it signifies?

S Clearly not.

F Well, how many words are in this line of Virgil: "If gods decree nothing from High City [Troy] remain . . ."[2]

S Eight.

F Requiring eight signs, right?

S They must.

F I presume you understand what the line is saying?

S Well enough, I suppose.

F Then tell me what each word, separately, signifies.

S Of course I know what *if* means, though I cannot come up with another word for it.

F Do you, then, understand what the word means when you come across it in context?

S *If*, I suppose, indicates indeterminacy, and where can that exist but in the mind?

F That will do for now. What of the other words?

S What can *nothing* mean but what does not exist?

F You may be right, but I hesitate to affirm it because of your earlier assent that every sign must have something it signifies—but what does not exist is not a something. So the third word in this line, since it does not signify a something, must not be a sign; and we must have been in error when we agreed either that every word is a sign, or that each sign has something it signifies.

S You have me on the ropes, I grant; but if a word has nothing it signifies, a man would be a fool to use it—and since you are talking to me, and I do not suspect you of making random noises, but of using words meant to advance my understanding, you would not have pronounced *these* two syllables [no-thing] if they did not signify something. If you chose them to elicit something by their sound in my ears, or to make me recall something, then you must know what I am trying to say, though I cannot formulate it.

F How shall we put it then?—perhaps that the word does not signify a thing that does not exist, but signifies our state of mind when we perceive that it does not exist, or think we perceive it.

S That may be just what I was trying to maintain.

F Well, let's in any case move on or we risk looking silly.

S How so?

F Breaking down because nothing got in our way.

S Embarrassing, all right. I don't see how it happened to us—but it clearly has.

4

F Perhaps, with God's help, we may untie this knot later on. Meanwhile, go back to Virgil's line, to define the other words in it.

S Well, the fifth word is *of*, for which I suppose we could substitute *from*.

F That is not what I was after—that for a familiar word you substitute an equally familiar one with the same meaning (if indeed it does have the same meaning, which we'll stipulate for now). Obviously, if the poet had said "from High City" rather than "of High City," you could have told me that *from* means *of*, since the two are equivalent in your eyes. But I am looking for the one reality, whatever that may be, that these two signify.

S I think *from* signifies a withdrawal of something from its former place; we say it is "from" there, whether the place no longer exists (as Troy does not in the verse) or whether it does (as we say that traveling merchants in Africa are "from" Rome).

F Even if I accept your examples (though I could perhaps give a number of counterexamples), you must admit that you are explaining words with other words, signs with other signs— that is, the obvious with the obvious. But I am after the reality signified by these signs.

5

S You surprise me by not recognizing, or pretending not to recognize, that I simply cannot do what you are asking. We are carrying on this very conversation by words, yet you keep asking me for things that, whatever they are, are *not* words—and you have asked for them in words of your own. If you want answers without words, then ask questions without words.

F Your point is well taken, yet if I use a word of three syllables, *partition*, and ask what they mean, couldn't you point with your finger, and I would instantly recognize what is meant by the three syllables, though you spoke nothing as you showed me what they meant?

S Of course that's possible, but only with words for physical objects, and for ones that are here to be pointed at.

F How about colors—are they physical objects, or aspects of the objects?

S The latter.

F Can't we point out colors? And if so, do you think that aspects of physical objects, along with the objects themselves, can be signified without using words so long as they are here?

S When I said physical objects, I was trying to indicate anything physical—everything, that is, that the body can sense.

F Look again—isn't there an exception to what you say?

S Oh yes—I should have said everything visible, not everything physical. I realize that sound, odor, taste, weight, heat, and other things are grasped by the senses, but cannot be identified by pointing at them.

F Yet you have seen men converse in a way with deaf people merely by gesturing; and the deaf themselves, using nothing but gestures, ask and answer questions, inform others, expressing everything (or almost everything) they wish to. In their case, your sounds and tastes and such, and not visible things alone, are indicated without words. Often, in fact, mimes narrate and explain whole stories without using words.

S True enough, but still—your mime cannot, any more than I can, show without words what *from* means.

6

F Perhaps not—but even if he could, whatever he might do to dance out the word's meaning would be just another sign for the thing, not the thing itself. He will still, that is, be indicating one sign with another sign (though not one word with another word)—so that his motions and the word *from* both indicate the same reality [which is neither of them]. And that reality itself, not any sign of it, is what I want to be shown.

S But how, I ask you, can such a thing be shown?

F As we showed the partition.

S But even that could not be shown without a sign, as the course of our argument has made clear—for the finger pointed at the wall is not the wall, but a sign directing one's attention to the wall. So I still do not see how anything can be shown without a sign.

F Well, if I should ask you what *walking* means, and you got up and showed me, wouldn't you be teaching by means of the thing itself, and not by words or other signs?

S I would, and it embarrasses me not to have anticipated a response so obvious, one that suggests at once a million other examples of things that can be shown directly and not by words—eating, for instance, or drinking, sitting, standing, shouting, and so on.

F Well, take another case. If I, having no idea what the word *walking* means, should ask you what it means, and you were already walking when I asked, how would you show me?

S I would keep on walking, but speed my pace, and what I did in response to your question would answer you, and I would not be using anything but the action itself to explain itself.

F Isn't hurrying different from walking? One who walks is not necessarily hurrying, nor does one have to walk at all in order to hurry—we say that one can read or write, or do all kinds of things, in a hurry. So if you just speed up what you are already doing when I ask you what walking is, I might be fooled into thinking that walking means hurrying, since that is what you added to your action.

S Then I admit we cannot show a thing without a sign if we happen to be doing the thing when we are asked. If we do not do something different, but continue what we were doing, the questioner will think we are ignoring him, and he will be insulted. If, however, he asks us to demonstrate an action we can perform on the spot, but don't happen to be performing when he asks, then we can show him what his word means by matching our action to his question, and no words will have been used—unless, of course, he asks me what talking is while we are talking. Then, no matter what I say in order to answer him, I'll have to keep on talking. But no matter how long it takes to make clear what talking means, I shall not be departing from the thing itself, to rely on signs instead of it, since talking is itself the thing at issue.

7

F   Neatly put. Are we agreed, then, that a thing can be shown without signs if we can answer a question with a corresponding action (but only if we are not already performing the action), or when we are asked about signs that we *are* making at the moment—for then we can speak on and continue to signify, since speech is itself a sign?

S   Agreed.

F   When [1] the question is about signs, therefore, it can be answered with signs; but if it is about things that are not signs, it can be answered either [2] with a corresponding action, if that can be performed on the spot, or [3] by drawing attention to the thing with signs.

S   So it seems.

F   Of these three then, consider first explaining signs with signs. Are words the only signs?

S   By no means.

F When we talk, it seems, we use words either to signify other words or other signs (for when we say "gesture" or "letter," those too are signs, along with the words we use of them), or we use words to signify things that are not signs—as when we say "a rock," a word that is a sign itself but that signifies what is clearly not a sign. This latter category, in which we use words as signs of things that are not signs, takes us astray, since we said we were first considering the signs of signs, and we can establish two kinds of these, namely the signs with which we teach or remind people of [the meaning of] the signs being used, or those that deal with other signs. Is that right?

S Surely.

8

F Tell me, then, what physical sense do words address.

S Hearing.

F What do gestures address?

S Sight.

F What if the words are written down—do they remain words, or become signs of words? If words are, properly speaking, vocal noises that articulate some meaning, and if vocal noises address the sense of hearing, then a written word, which addresses sight, is a sign directed at the eyes for bringing to mind a sign directed at the ears.

S My view precisely.

F Do you agree, too, that a noun is the sign of something?

S I do.

F   A sign of what?

S   Of an entity that can be named—Romulus, for instance, or Rome, virtue, river, and so on.

F   So the four nouns you give signify certain things?

S   Of course.

F   Is there any difference between the nouns and the things they signify?

S   A great difference.

F   Namely?

S   In the first place, the nouns are signs, the things named are not.

F   Could we give the name "signifiables" to the things that can be designated by signs but are not signs themselves, as we call things that can be seen "seeables"—to refer to them more conveniently?[3]

S   All right.

F   Can your four nouns, which are signs, be signified themselves by other signs?

S   I haven't forgotten already that we saw a difference between spoken words and written words, the former signs, the latter signs of signs.

F   And what makes them different?

S   The written are seeable, the spoken are hearable—why not admit a new term like hearable if we have already used signifiable?

F   That's fine with me. But I'm asking if your four nouns can be indicated by different hearable signs, as you said they could by seeable signs.

S Well, as I said a while back that a noun signifies a thing, and gave four examples, that must entail that both "noun" and the four specific nouns, when pronounced aloud, are [different] hearables.

F Then, since both the seeable and the hearable signs are similar as signs, how are they dissimilar?

S One difference is that the word *noun* is a hearable sign of other hearable things, but the four examples are signs of things, not of other signs—though some of the things signified are themselves seeable (like Romulus, Rome, and river), while others are only thinkable (like virtue).

9

F Fine—now, do you accept the definition of *word* as any vocal noise articulated to convey meaning?

S I do.

F So *noun*, since it is a vocal noise with meaning, is itself a word, and when we say that an eloquent man uses fine words, he must be using nouns—as when the slave in Terence tells his master, "Use fine words of me," he might have said "fine nouns."

S He might.

F Then you see that when we pronounce the single syllable "word," we are also pronouncing a noun, and the word is a sign of the noun?

S That follows.

F Then tell me this. You hold, on the one hand, that a word signifies a noun, that a noun can signify a river, and that *river* can signify a visible thing; and you also hold that there is a difference between the seeable thing and the word *river*, which is its sign; and also between that word and *noun*, which is a sign of the sign—but what, precisely, is the difference between the sign for the word *noun* and the sign that the word is?

S I see this difference at least. A thing signified by a word can, it is true, be signified by a noun as well—a noun is a word, but so is river a word. But what is signified by a word is not always signifiable by a noun. The *if*, for instance, at the beginning of the verse you brought up, or the *from*, from which we derived the long mental exercise that has brought us to this point, are both words, but not nouns. And there are many such. Since every noun is a word, but not every word is a noun, I find this difference between them—that a word is the sign of a thing that does not signify other signs; whereas a noun is the sign of a thing that can signify other things.

F As you would say that a horse is an animal, but not every animal is a horse?

S Exactly.

F So the difference between noun and word is the same as between horse and animal [pause]—or do you hold back from making this equation because a *verb* with its tenses (like "I am writing, I wrote," or "I am reading, I read") is also called a word [*verbum*], though it is not a noun?

S That did puzzle me.

F Don't let it. Anything signifying another thing we can call a sign, and words are just one example of that. Military insignia are also signs, but not verbal ones.4 So if I tell you that, just as every horse is an animal, but not every animal is a horse, every word [*verbum*] is a sign, but not every sign is a word, would you still be puzzled?

S No, I can agree that words in general differ from a noun as animals in general differ from a horse.

10

F Are you just as certain that the three-syllable word *animal*, when we pronounce it, is different from the thing it refers to?

S Yes, I said that—a sign is different from what it signifies.

F Then you hold the corollary that all signs are signs of something other than themselves—as the three syllables we sound out as *animal* are not themselves an animal?

S Certainly not, but when we say "sign," we refer not only to other signs, whatever they may be, but to itself, since sign is a word, and words are signs.

F Doesn't what you say about "sign" apply as well to "word," since when we say that single syllable, we mean whatever is articulated with meaning, and that describes itself as well?

S Yes it does.

F And cannot the same be said of "noun"? For while it refers to nouns of any gender, it is itself a noun of the neuter gender [an "it"], and if I asked you what part of speech it is, could you give any other answer than that it is, itself, a noun?

S None at all.

F So some signs are signs not only of other things but of themselves.

S True.

F Could we say the same thing about the three-syllable word *conjunction?*

S Not quite, since what it *signifies* is not a noun, though *it* is a noun.

11

F You see my point already—that though some signs are interchangeable, the first meaning the second, the second the first, we cannot say the same thing about the three-syllable word *conjunction*—since it denotes words like *if, because, or, since, except, so, therefore,* and the like; and none of them means our three-syllable word, yet it means all of them.

S If that is the case, I would like to know what signs are interchangeable.

F Have you noticed that in using the terms *word* and *noun* we were using two words?

S Certainly.

F And in using them we were using, as well, two nouns?

S That, too.

F Thus a noun can be signified by a word, a word by a noun.

S Exactly.

F Can you say, then, how they differ—apart from their diverse spelling and pronunciation?

S Yes—I just made the point a moment ago. When we say

word, we mean any vocal noise that conveys a meaning. Thus every noun, and even the word *noun* itself, when we pronounce it, is a word; but not every word is a noun, even though any word, including *word*, is a noun when we pronounce it.

12

F If someone claimed that every noun is a word, and every word a noun, could you find some difference between them, apart from the sound of the letters in each?

S I doubt that I could, or that there would be any other difference.

F Even if every vocal noise with any meaning were both a word and a noun, but designated a word for one use and a noun for another, would there still be no difference?

S Not that I can see.

F Yet you will admit that all colored things are seeable, and all seeable things colored, yet the two words are different and have different meanings?

S Yes.

F How if, in the same way, though every word is a noun, and every noun a word, whether considered as two words or two nouns, they should still have different meanings?

S I suppose that could be, though I don't see how—no doubt you will explain.

F You admit, of course, that if any vocal noise, one conveying meaning, is pronounced by the lips, it whirs in the ears to be heard, and stirs memory to be known?

S Clearly.

F So two different operations occur when we say any word.

S They do.

F What if the very names of these two should be derived from this difference, *word* from "whirred" and *noun* from "known," so that the first is rightly named for the ear, the second for the mind?⁵

13

S I will concede that, if you first prove that every word is a noun.

F You remember from your grammar lessons that a pronoun is what takes the place of a noun, giving it a briefer designation? Isn't that the definition you had to recite for your schoolmaster: "A pronoun is that part of speech which takes the place of a noun, expressing the same thing as the noun does, but more briefly"?

S Yes, an excellent definition.

F Then it follows that, by this definition, pronouns can exist only with reference to their nouns, of which alone they can take the place. When we say this man, the king himself, the same woman, this gold, or that silver, the words *this, himself, the same, this,* and *that* are pronouns, while the words *man, king, woman, gold,* and *silver* are the nouns, which have a fuller meaning than their pronouns.

S I see that, yes.

F Give me, then, a few conjunctions.

S All right—*and, moreover, but, yet.*

F   Haven't you made a mistake? Aren't those nouns?

S   Certainly not.

F   So when I asked "Aren't those," was my grammar wrong?

S   Not at all—and *touché* for showing me how they have to be nouns, to be called "those" in the sentence. But I still have misgivings. Without denying that you used "those" correctly, since the conjunctions can, I admit, be nouns, nonetheless "those" may be properly used because it implies "those *words*," and if you ask me what part of speech "words" are, I say *it* is a noun. Use of the pronoun for noun is proper because it *implies* the noun.

14

F   Clever, but a fallacy. To escape it, follow me closely—if I can succeed in making it clear. To handle words with words is to interweave them like interlaced fingers: rubbing them together makes it hard to tell, except by each finger on its own, which is doing the itching and which the scratching.

S   After that comparison I am *really* paying attention.

F   Then (to invoke the authority that stands highest with us) when Paul the Apostle says, "With Christ there is no Is and is not, only an Is" [2 Corinthians 1.19], I doubt that we are to think the two letters of "Is" *are* Christ, but he is what the two syllables stand for.[6]

S   Clearly.

F   So when the Apostle says "With Christ there is an Is," that is equivalent to saying "What is *called* an Is was with Christ." If he had said, "There is power in Christ," that would be equivalent to "What is called power is in Christ." The two syllables we pronounce as "power" are not in Christ, what the syllables stand for is in him.

S I see that.

F Then you must see that there is no difference between saying "what is *called* power" and "what is *named* power."

S None at all.

F And no more difference in saying "what is called an Is" and "what is named an Is."

S I see that too.

F So you know where we are going?

S Not quite.

F You don't deny that a thing's name is its noun.

S Yes, that's obvious.

F Then Is is a noun when it names him.

S Inescapably.

F Yet if I had asked you what part of speech *is* is, you would, I think, have told me it is a verb, not a noun, though now we are discovering it is a noun.

S You have me there.

F Then the other parts of speech must also be nouns, by this line of reasoning.

S Yes, considered only as signifiers. But if you ask about the signified things they refer to, as named by them, what can I say, but that they name different parts of speech and not nouns, however your argument tries to make them nouns?

15

F Does it bother you that someone might argue that the apostle Paul has a command of reality but not of verbal usage, so that the basis for our demonstration is less solid than we proposed, and that Paul was sound in his living and teaching but not necessarily in his command of language when he said, "With him is an Is"—remember that he himself admitted he was "not gifted in speaking" [2 Corinthians 11.6]. Could you mount an answer?

S I am not ready for him myself, but I hope you can call on some champion arguer who will do what you have in mind.

F But can't reason alone, without appeal to authority, show that all parts of speech are signs of something; and if signified by them, then named by them; and if named by them, then named with a noun—something true not only of our language but of others, since it is obvious that if you ask *what* Greeks use for our "who," they would answer *tis;* if what they use for "wish," the answer is *thelein;* if for "written down," it is *gegrammenon;* for "and" it is *kai,* for "from" *apo,* for "alas," it is *oi*—and so on through all parts of speech which I have referred to, rightly asking *what,* which could only be done if a *noun* is demanded. That is why Paul spoke accurately and we can uphold him without calling on any verbal champions—is there anything they could add to make our position any firmer?

16

But if someone too weak of mind or strong of will should resist this reasoning, and demand some super-lexicographer to lay down the law of of verbal usage, what greater Latinist could there be than Cicero? He, in the famed Verrine speeches, called "among" a noun, though it is a preposition in grammar. Perhaps I misunderstand the passage, and I or another will later advance a different interpretation of it—but this much, I think, none can deny: masters of grammar teach that a complete sentence (what Cicero calls a proposition) contains a *subject* asserted or denied by a *verb*, and they correctly say that when the verb is in the third person, the subject must be in the nominative case—so that if I say "The man is sitting" or "The horse is running," you will recognize that I have formed two propositions.

S Surely.

F And you can distinguish the two sentences' subjects, man and horse, as well as what they were doing, as shown in the verbs—sitting in the one case, running in the other.

S Yes.

F So if I said "is sitting" or "is running," you would rightly inquire of me who or what was doing these things, and I would answer either a man, or a horse, or some animal, or whatever, anything to join the verb and complete a statement, an affirmation or a denial.

S Right.

F Take it a stage further, and imagine we are looking at something far off, unable to see whether it is an animal or a rock or whatever, and I said to you, "That must be an animal, since it is a man," wouldn't I just be babbling?

S   In that particular case, of course. But it would not be babbling to say, "That must be an animal if it is a man."

F   You make the right distinction—your *if* is right in my view as well as yours, and my *because* is wrong for both of us.

S   We are agreed.

F   Did I use complete sentences when I said "*if* is right" and "*because* is wrong"?

S   Yes.

F   Then give me the sentences' subjects and verbs.

S   The verbs are "is" in "is right" and "is wrong," which leaves "if" and "because" as the nouns.

F   Thus proving that the two conjunctions are also nouns.

S   Entirely.

F   Can you use the same method on your own to show that all other parts of speech are nouns?

S   I can.

17

F   Moving on, then, tell me whether you would equate nouns and *terms*, just as we have equated nouns and words.

S   They do seem the same, apart from their syllables' different sound.

F   That's good enough for now, though some *do* find a difference in their meaning. In any case, as you have noticed, we are now dealing with signs that signify each other, without any distinction except for different pronunciation of their sounds, and we say that each can signify other parts of speech as well.

S I don't get that.

F Do you get this—that noun means term and term means noun; that the two do not differ except in pronunciation, so far as a noun is a noun; but that they do differ insofar as a noun is a grammatical part of speech [and term is not]?

S Oh. Yes.

F That is all I mean by word and term signifying each other.

18

S That is clear enough, but I still wonder what you meant by saying that they can "signify other parts of speech as well."

F Didn't our argument show that all parts of speech can be called either nouns or terms, and both words will refer to them all?

S It did.

F How about "noun" considered as the sound of a single syllable, what would you call it if I asked? Wouldn't you answer that it is itself a noun?

S Of course.

F But when we call a conjunction by its three-syllable name, that noun does not include the thing it signifies.

S I can see that.

F That is why I said that a noun signifies not only itself but the other parts of speech as well—and *term* acts the same.

S Clear enough—and now it comes to me that *noun* can be either general or specific, but *term* is not one of the grammatical parts of speech, so this sets it apart from *noun*, along with their difference in sound.

F How about *noun* and *onoma*? Does anything set them apart but the fact that one is in our language and the other in Greek?

S Nothing that I can see.

F So we end up with four kinds of signs—signs that mean themselves; signs that mean each other; signs that refer to the same thing; and signs that have no difference but their pronunciation—the latter we have just turned up, and the first three we said could be understood as either nouns or words.

S That covers it.

19

F Would you run over, then, what we have established so far?

S I can try. First we spent some time inquiring why we talk to each other, and we answered, either to teach someone or to recall something; that when we ask a question, it is to teach another what we want; that when we are singing only for our own enjoyment, we are not talking as such; that in prayers addressed to God (who, we realize, cannot be informed or reminded of anything), we use words only to remind ourselves or so that others may be reminded or informed by us.

Then, after it was agreed that words are nothing but signs, and that what does not mean something beyond itself is not a sign, you presented me with a verse, and asked me to give, if I could, the meaning for each separate word. It runs, "If gods decree nothing from High City remain," and though the fourth word is familiar and clear, we could not determine what it means. When I observed that we could not be using it without a point, but must mean to convey something by it, you said that it might indicate the attitude of mind when one expects to find that a thing exists but finds instead (or thinks he finds) that it does not exist. But then you put off with a pun any probing of this mystery (whatever it may be), saving it for another time—do you think I have forgotten you still owe me that explanation?

While I was trying to state the meaning of the fifth word [from], you pressed me not to explain one word by its synonym but to show the thing it signifies. When I said that could not be done in an exchange of words, we turned to things that can be shown a questioner by pointing at them—I thought these would all be physical objects, but we agreed that it meant all seeable things. From this we moved somehow or other to deaf people and mimes, who could indicate by bodily signs not only all seeable things, but many other things as well—in fact, almost everything we describe with words—though we agreed that even such bodily actions make up a system of signs.

Then we returned to the inquiry whether things represented by signs could be presented without signs, since even the act of pointing, to a partition or a color or anything seeable, is itself a sign. Here I made the mistake of saying that such a signless answer cannot be given, though at length we worked it out that one can answer a question with an action if we are not performing the act while being questioned, and can then perform it as the answer. But even here there is an exception—talking, since we can tell a questioner what talking is even while we continue to talk, a matter easily enough put in words.

20

So we were now agreeing that there are signs representing other signs, signs signifying things that are not signs, and even things we can signify without signs—by action in response to a question. The first one we went into more thoroughly and it emerged that some signs cannot be signified by the sign they signify, as is the case with the trisyllable *conjunction*. But other signs can, as when we say *sign* we signify *word*, and vice versa, since signs and words are each of them both sign and word.

But in this category of signs that signify each other, some do so as equivalents, others as nonequivalent, and a third group as identical with each other. For when we pronounce the monosyllable *sign* we refer to everything it can signify and to everything that signifies it. But when we say *word*, that is not a sign of all other signs, but only of vocal noises shaped to convey meaning. Thus, though the monosyllable *word* and the monosyllable *sign* can refer to each other, *sign* has greater scope than does *word*, one monosyllable covering more than the other one does.

But word and noun, in their widest use, are to some

extent equivalent—our discussion showed that all parts of speech can be nouns, since pronouns can refer to them, proving they are the names for something—and, besides, they can all be made the subject of a sentence by addition of a verb to them. Still, though noun and word are to some extent equivalent, in that each word is a noun, each noun a word, yet they are not exact equivalents—in fact, it is highly probable, according to our exchange, that they have different etymologies, word coming from "whirred" in the ear, noun from "known" in the mind—that is why, when we want to lodge a thing in our inner mind, we properly ask what its name is, and only rarely what its word sounds like.

There are, finally, signs not only nearly equivalent but entirely identical, differing only in their pronunciation, like noun and [Greek] *onoma*. Oh, and one thing I almost forgot—the thing in this category I had not seen: that when signs signify each other, each signifies itself as well as other things. This is as much as I can remember. Since I think your order of exposition was logical and clear, you will judge whether my account of it was as well arranged.

21

F   You remember everything I was asking for—in fact, I admit that I understand better, after your summary, things we were trying to dig out of their dark crannies by study and conversation.7 But it is hard to say, at this point, what goal we are moving toward through this labyrinth. I hope you don't think we are just playing intellectual games, diverting ourselves from important matters with childish quibbles of little or no practical import. Or if you suspect that our discussion is laboring to bring forth something worthy, you must by now have wanted to know what it is, or to get some hint of it. I want to assure you I did not start this discussion to make low puns. We may be having some fun while we are at it, but not of a sort to be despised as childish, since these are not trivial or indifferent things we are weighing. I am trying to prove there is a life that is blessed, one (moreover) that is eternal, which we might achieve if God (who is Truth) assists our feeble steps in ways that suit them, and I hope you won't think I started such a journey from an inappropriate point, not looking to things themselves but to their signs. Do you see that I am leading you into the subject, not with light games but with limbering-up exercises for the mind, to equip us not only for breathing the rare bright air of the blessed life but for making our home in it?[8]

S Forge on, as before—I don't think anything you say or do is trivial.

22

F Go back, then, to a thing that is signified by a sign but is not itself a sign. And first tell me whether the masculine is masculine.[9]

S Now I fear you *are* playing games with me.

F How?

S By seriously asking whether the masculine is masculine.

F Would you still think I am playing games if I ask you

whether the first syllable of that word is *mas,* the second *cu,* the third *line?*

F   Yes.

F   Yet you would not deny that the three syllables, taken to-gether, mean masculine?

S   Who could?

F   And what if I ask are *you* those three syllables?

S   Oh, I see where you are going—no, I am not.

F   Then tell me, so you will not think I am playing games with you.

S   You want me to say I am not masculine.

F   Why not, since you have granted all the premises to the question?

S   I cannot say what I think until I learn from you whether your question was whether I am the *three syllables* or the *thing* they signify.

F   It was for you to say which question you are answering. If my query could be taken two ways, you should have rec-ognized that fact, and asked which was at issue before you responded.

S   Why should the two senses bother me, since I would answer both the same way—whether we are talking about the three syllables of the word, or the real thing the word refers to, masculine is masculine in either case.

F   True enough—but why did you take the word *masculine* in two senses, but not the rest of my sentence?

S   What makes you think I did that?

F   Well, first of all, if you thought my first question only sounded out three syllables, you should not have answered me at all, under the opinion that I was not even asking a question [just making three sounds]. But when I put the three syllables in a context, asking "whether the masculine is masculine," the context made you think not of the three-syllable sign, but of what it signifies—as is clear from the promptitude with which you assumed you knew the answer to the question.

S   That's right.

F   Then why did you take only the single word as both a sound and as a sign?

S   But now let me take the word in its context, as dealing only with what it signifies. Let us agree that we cannot hold discourse at all unless our minds are directed by the sound of words to the things they indicate. Show me then, how I was tricked by a line of argument leading to the conclusion that I am not masculine.

F   Instead, I'll repeat my questions, so you can see for yourself where you went astray.

S   All right.

23

F   I won't repeat the opening question, since you have already answered it. But consider this point more accurately—does the syllable *mas* refer to anything beyond itself, or the syllable *cu*, or the syllable *line?*

S None that I see at the moment.

F But when you put them together, the masculine comes into being.

S Not at all, for we agreed, and did so on good footing, that we should treat signs in terms of the *things* they refer to, and affirm or deny what is said of *them*, but those three syllables, taken separately, do not signify anything and have to be treated merely as sounds.

F You take the position, then, on the basis of principle, that answers to questions should address only what the words refer to [not the words themselves]?

S Provided we are dealing with compete words [not just syllables], I do not see what other position could be taken.

F Then I would like to hear you refute the man who used the common joke to argue that a lion came out of his opponent's mouth. Having asked the man whether what we say comes out of our mouth, and won agreement on that, he easily maneuvered him into saying *lion*, and then began to fleer and insist that, having admitted that whatever we say comes out of our mouth, and that he undeniably did say lion, the good fellow spewed out a bad beast.

S Refuting such a buffoon would be no trouble at all. I just deny his premise, that whatever we say comes out of our mouth. We speak to signify something, and the signified thing does not come from our mouth, only its sign—unless a sign is precisely what we are signifying, as we said before.

24

F   The fellow would be no match for you. But still—how do
you answer me when I ask is *masculine* an adjective?

S   It is.

F   Then I must see an adjective when I look at you?

S   No.

F   Need I draw the conclusion?

S   Please don't. I admitted that I am not masculine when I answered you that masculine is an adjective. But I thought it
was our understanding that we should affirm or deny what
is said according to what it refers to.

F   Yet even your mistaking my question was instructive. You
were confused by the very way our mind works. If I should
ask you, "What is masculine," you could answer "a gender";
but if I asked what part of speech is masculine, the only correct answer you could give is "an adjective." Thus since
masculine is both a gender and an adjective, the first answer
addresses what is signified, the second addresses the sign.
Whoever, then, asks whether masculine is an adjective, I
would have to say yes, since he has made it clear that he is
considering the word precisely as a sign. But if, instead, he
asks simply what is masculine, it is even easier to answer
him—if he makes no distinction between sign and thing
signified, asking simply what is masculine, the mind inclines
naturally, by the structure of language itself, to what the
three syllables signify, and there is no appropriate response
except to say *gender*, or even to give a complete definition,

as "one of the two divisions of sexual animals." Do you agree?

S Entirely. But if, nonetheless, we grant that masculine is also an adjective, how do we escape the uncomfortable claim that we are not masculine?

F How otherwise than by showing that the answer did not fit the terms of the question as asked? Or if the questioner insists on an answer in terms of the sign [not the thing itself], why should I be bothered in admitting that I am not three syllables, which is all he means by masculine?

S That is all true, but why, in that case, is it annoying to hear, "You are not masculine," when all I am admitting is that I am not three syllables?

F Because it is hard not to refer the three syllables as they are being spoken to the thing they signify, so natural is it in most cases for the mind to go immediately to their significance.

S That must be the case.

25

F Now I ask you to concede that what is signified is more to be esteemed than is its sign. A thing that exists for the sake of something else is of necessity inferior to that other thing, is it not?

S I'm not sure. *Ordure,* for instance, is a word worthier than what it refers to. What repels us it not the sound of the word, since it is, with a slight change, the same as *order*— but think of the vast difference between the things signified.[10] So I would never attribute to the sign what we find offensive in the signified, but would prefer the former, affecting our ears, to the latter, affecting our noses.

F You are quick on the uptake. But are you really denying that signs are inferior to the things they signify?

S That's my opinion.

F Then why do you think men bothered to create a word for such a vile and contemptible thing? Or do you think it was wrong of them to do so?

S I cannot call them wrong or right, since I do not know what they had in mind.

F Do you know why you, at least, use the word?

S Of course—because I use this sign to teach or remind another, when I address him, what I think he should learn or remember.

F And the knowledge or remembrance, made possible only by this word, is that not worthier than the word itself?

S Admittedly the knowledge is better than the word, but the word is still better than the thing.

26

F Going back to my general rule, even if not everything is to be preferred to its sign, it remains true that everything that exists for the sake of something else is inferior to that something else. The knowledge of *ordure*, for the sake of which the word was created, is just as superior to the word as the thing itself, according to your claim, is inferior to the word. We say that knowledge conveyed is superior to the word conveying it because the word was created for the knowledge, not the knowledge for the word. Thus when a certain glutton—a "belly worshiper," as the Apostle would put it [Romans 16.18]—said that he lived in order to eat, a more disciplined man replied in disgust, "Better, rather, to eat in order to live." Yet both men were applying the same norm. The first disgusted the other because he thought so little of his life as to make it exist only to gratify his belly, having no other reason for living than to eat. And the other man deserves praise simply for reversing the rank of things, affirming that we eat to live rather than live to eat.

In the same way, if some talkative lover of his own voice should say, "I teach others in order to talk with them," you (or any person not dull to the real worth of things) might respond, "Talking in order to teach is surely better, sir." If these things are true, and you know they are, how can you deny that words are less important than the things for which we employ the words; that this use of words is itself preferable to the words themselves; that words exist only for their usefulness; and that their usefulness is for teaching. The test that makes teaching better than talking is the same that makes talking better than words. For knowing is better than the words by which one knows. If you have anything to counter this, I would like to hear it.

27

S I go along with you when you say that knowing is better than the words by which we know, but I do not know if that justifies your more general claim that anything that exists for the sake of another thing is necessarily inferior to it.

F Let's probe that matter further when we have more time. What you have admitted so far is sufficient for my present point, since you grant that knowledge of reality is worthier than knowledge of its sign. Then knowledge of the former should be preferred to knowledge of the latter, should it not?

S When did I grant that knowledge of the signified is not only better than knowledge of the sign but than the sign itself? That is what I would be conceding if I agreed with your last statement. What if the name of ordure is not only better than the thing, but knowledge of the name is better than knowledge of the thing, though the name is inferior to knowledge of the name? There are, after all, four things in play—the name, the thing named, knowledge of the name, and knowledge of the thing. If the first is superior to the second, why should the third not also be superior to the fourth—or be its equal if not its superior?

28

F The way you not only remember what you conceded, but defend each of your positions, is admirable, I concede. But even you, I bet, must realize that the monosyllable *sin* is, as we pronounce it, better than what it stands for; yet knowing about the word is not as important as knowing about sin. Admittedly, of the four things you list for our consideration—the name, the thing named, knowledge of the name, and knowledge of the thing—the first is justly thought superior to the second. When Persius, for instance, uses sin in a poem [3.32], calling a person "by sin dumbfounded," the word *sin* does not make the poem sinful but gives it in fact a certain elegance. But when the reality symbolized by the word is found in a person [not a poem], it makes him sinful. So the third of your four items is not [as you say] superior to the fourth, but inferior to it. Knowing about the word *sin* is not as important as knowing about sin.

S   Would you still prefer such knowledge when it makes men miserable? Didn't Persius himself say [3.35–38] that the agony of men who know all the sins they cannot escape is greater than any inflicted by a tyrant or by their own evil cravings?

F   By that line of argument, knowing the name of virtue would be superior to knowing virtue itself, since knowing virtue without having it is a torture—is indeed the very one Persius wished upon tyrants.

S   God keep me from so crazed a view. Now I see that knowledge itself is not to be blamed [for the sinner's suffering], since the highest moral discipline enlightens our soul with it, but that those should be called most wretched—I think Persius really meant this—who are so subject to sin that not even healing knowledge can help them.

F   You put the matter well. But what care we how Persius is to be interpreted? We are not accountable in such grave matters to poetic sentiment. And it is no simple matter to sort out what forms of knowledge are preferable. It is hard enough to have reached our present position—namely, that knowledge of a signified is superior to its sign, though it may not be superior to *knowledge* of its sign. So let us go farther and deeper into our earlier discussion of things that can be shown without signs but by enactment, as we saw in the case of walking, sitting, and the like.

S Oh yes, I remember.

29

F Do you think all the actions we might perform in answer to a question reveal a thing without the use of signs, or do some fail to do that?

S Mulling it over, I cannot now find a single thing demonstrable without a symbol—unless perhaps talking, or the act of explaining when that is what is asked for. For I see that any act performed in answer to a question cannot of itself show what is being asked for. If someone, to take our earlier example, asks me what walking is, when I am not doing anything, or doing something else, were I to walk at once, trying to show him what he asked about, how do I know he will not take the *distance* I walk as the answer to his question, and be misled by that interpretation, so he thinks that someone going farther than I did, or less far, is therefore not walking? And what I say about this word holds true for all the things I thought could be demonstrated without a symbol—with the two possible exceptions I brought up.

30

F Fair enough so far. [But about those two things,] would you say talking is different from teaching?

S They must be—if they were the same, no one could teach without talking. But since we can teach by signs other than words, who can doubt that they differ?

F Do teaching and signifying mean the same thing?

S I believe so.

F If it were claimed that we make signs in order to teach, would you agree?

S Surely.

F So if one, on the contrary, said that we teach in order to make signs, wouldn't the general rule we reached be enough to refute him?

S Yes.

F And since we use signs in order to teach, not vice versa, teaching must be something different from making signs.

S That's right—I was wrong to equate them.

F Then answer this: when one teaches what teaching is, does he do this with signs or in some other way?

S How else?

F Then you were wrong as well when you said, earlier, that if one asked what teaching is, that could be taught without using signs. Now we see that this is impossible, since you have admitted that making signs and teaching are distinct things. If, as it appears, they differ, and teaching cannot be demonstrated without using signs, then teaching cannot be demonstrated by itself, as you said. So nothing at all can be demonstrated by itself, except for speaking—and since it *is* a sign, then *nothing* can be demonstrated without a sign.

S I see no flaw in that.

31

F We have established, then, that nothing can be taught without signs, and that the knowledge which is conveyed by the signs is worthier than the signs—though it is possible that some of the things signified are not superior to their signs.

S So it seems.

F Does it seem to you that we have taken a wind-about journey to a trivial objective? For ever since we began this verbal jousting, which has gone on so long, we have been working to discover three things only—whether anything can be taught without signs; whether signs are to be preferred to what they signify; and whether the knowledge of the signified is preferable to its sign. But I would like to raise this fourth brief point with you—whether what we have discovered so far you can affirm as beyond question.

S I would hope we gained some certitude through paths so dubious and difficult, but something about your question troubles me, and makes me leery of a confident reply. I suspect you would not have asked me if you did not have something in reserve to spring on me, and the very complexity of such matters eludes my grasp of them as a whole and keeps me from giving an assured answer, for fear that something lurks in their depths that my mind, for all its effort, has not reached.

F I welcome your wariness, as evidence that you are not rash in your judgments—which can help you preserve a certain equanimity. For some uneasiness is almost inevitable when things we have been quick to accept as certain, are, by logical challenge, shaken to their foundations—wrenched, as it were, right out of our grasp. In proportion as it is safe to accept arguments well framed and tested, it is perilous to entertain unexamined propositions as if they were established—or else, when we see things undermined that we believed firmly built and permanent, we may develop a dislike or distrust of reason itself, as if there were no way of giving a sure consent even to the most evident truths.

32

Despite all that, let us rethink your withholding of consent to what we have so far concluded. I put it to you thus: if one unacquainted with the art of snaring birds, which is done with twigs and birdlime, should meet a bird catcher along the way, one outfitted with all the tools of his trade but not plying them at the moment, just walking along—suppose the observer should quicken his pace, puzzling out to himself what such strange equipment might mean, until the bird catcher, noticing the man's curiosity and wanting to demonstrate his skill, deploys his limed reeds, his rod, and his hawk when a little bird presents itself, using them to immobilize, manipulate, and bag the prize. Hasn't he taught the onlooker what he wanted to know, enacting the answer without any signs?

S I suspect we have the same problem we encountered in the case of a question about walking—and, besides, I doubt that the whole art of bird catching could be demonstrated by your example.

F Let's make it simple by stipulating that the observer in the example is so quick at understanding as to see the whole bird-catching art from this one display of it. For my contention it is enough that, in some cases (though not all), some men (though not all) might learn in this way without any signs being used.

S Then I would just stipulate a man so quick at understanding as to recognize the whole art of walking from the taking of a few steps.

F Stipulate away—I balk not at what you say, but welcome it, since it means that we have discovered together that some things can be demonstrated without the use of signs, and that our earlier conclusion that nothing can be demonstrated without signs was false—and not because one or two examples can be cited of such demonstration without signs, but because thousands can. Why, after all, should that surprise us? Putting aside the performances to be seen in any number of theaters, where actions are performed without the use of signs, what about the sun, streaming light over all things and luminously clothing them, or the moon and stars, the earth and the sea with all things bred in them, are they not revealed to us simply as we look at them, God and nature supplying them to our view?

33

We may in fact discover, if we press the matter closely, that nothing is demonstrated by its own signs. If a sign is shown to me before I know what it signifies, it can reveal nothing to me. But if I do know beforehand, what has it demonstrated on its own? When I read in the book of Daniel [3.94] that "their *sarabarae* were immune to harm," the word *sarabarae* means nothing to me. If someone suggests to me that the word refers to some kind of headgear, is he teaching me what head means, or what gear means? I already knew those things. And I did not learn them just because someone called them that, but when I saw them for myself. When the monosyllable pronounced as "head" first stirred in my ears, it meant as little to me as when I first heard or read *"sarabarae."* But when the word was said again and again, I began to take notice of it and to figure out where in conversation it was being used, until I connected the sound with something already familiar to me from sight. Before I made that connection, "head" was just a sound. It became a sign to me only when I recognized the *thing* it signified—so I learned not from the sign of the thing but from the sight of it. In this way, a sign is more to be learned from its object than the object is from it.

34

For a clearer grasp on the matter, suppose this case: we have just heard for the first time someone say "head." Since we do not know whether this sound is simply a noise or the sign of something, we ask what "head" is—remember, we are not yet asking *what* it signifies, but *whether* it signifies, which we cannot be sure of so long as we wonder whether it is a sign in the first place—and at this point someone points to the head. Seeing the thing, we learn that what we heard was a sign, a thing we could not have known earlier. There are two things involved in its being a sign, its sound and its sense, and the sound does not strike us as a sign but as a stirring in the ears, while its sense becomes apparent only as a sight—of the thing it symbolizes. The pointing of the finger cannot signify anything but the thing at which it is pointed, since it is not pointing to another sign but to the actual part of the body called its head. So the pointing does not give me knowledge of the head, which I already had, nor of the sign, at which it is not pointing.

The pointing, in fact, is not very important in itself, since it is more a sign of indicating than of the thing indicated— like the imperative "See!" with which we sometimes accompany our pointing, in case one sign of indication does not suffice. What I am trying to bring home to you, as best I can, is that we are not taught by the signs we call words. Rather, as I told you, the force of a word—that is, the meaning connected with its sound—we learn from the signified reality, which we already knew, rather than learning the reality from what signifies it.

35

Now what I said about the head applies also to gear, and to numberless other things I could cite. Yet my knowing these things would not, of itself, make me understand *sarabarae*. If someone were to describe what *sarabarae* are like by tracing one in the air or on a page, I will not say that he does not teach me (though, given some time, I could maintain that) but, more important for our present purpose, I maintain only that he did not teach me by words. Still, if we are both in the presence of *sarabarae* and he says, "See! *Sarabarae*," I would learn something I did not know before, not by any words that were said, but rather by looking at the thing, from the sight of which I learn and remember what the word refers to. For in learning about that thing, I did not rely on someone else's words but on my own eyes—though I may have relied on words to tell me what to look at, after which I saw it by myself.

36

The most, then, that can be said for the scope of words is that they afford us an occasion for examining something, but they do not demonstrate it to our understanding.[11] One who would really teach must bring before my eyes, or some other bodily sense, or the mind itself, that which I want to know. From words we learn nothing but other words, or rather their sound and accent. Since a word is by definition a sign, a word I hear is not even a word for me until I know what is signified by it.

So it is only from knowledge of the things they signify that words become signs, while from the sound of words alone we do not even know that they are words. We learn nothing new from words we already know, and we cannot testify to new knowledge from those we do not know until we learn what it is they signify, which is established not by the hearing of the sounds that carry them but from knowledge of the things they symbolize. The soundest rule, then, the whole summary of truth with regard to words, is that we either know what they signify or we do not. If we know that already, we are not taught it but remember it; and if we do not know that, then we cannot remember it, but may perhaps be directed to seek it.

37

You might say that we cannot truly understand *sarabarae*, the sound of whose name is all we now have in mind, unless we can visualize what it is, and we cannot know more about the word [than its sound] until we know about the headgear itself. Yet we recognize that the three young men [who wore the headgear in the book of Daniel] overcame the ruler and his fire by their faith and piety, sang praise to God, and earned praise even from their foe—and what but words taught us this? I answer that we already had stored in our mind what every one of those words symbolizes. I already knew what three young men are, and a furnace, and a fire, and a ruler, and what it is to be burnt by fire, and everything else conveyed by those words.

But the words Ananias, Azarias, and Misael are as strange to me as ever *sarabarae* was. And for knowing them the words themselves were no help, and could not be. That everything contained in scripture happened as it did in history is something that I rather believe than know—a distinction recognized by those we believe in, since the prophet Isaiah said [7.9] "Unless you believe, you will not understand." He could not have written that unless he understood the distinction. What I understand, I believe as well; though what I believe I do not necessarily understand. I know I need to believe some things I do not know—need, for instance, to believe the story of the three young men. Even where I cannot know, then, I need to believe without knowing.

38

As for all the things we do understand, we do not derive them from a speaker sounding words exterior to us, but from listening to the interior truth that informs our mind, however much words may provide us an occasion to consult that truth. The one we listen to there is the one who teaches us, the changeless power of God and his Wisdom never ending. Every creature that reasons is listening to him, but he responds according to each person's disposition toward him, as accepting or resisting him. If error occurs, it is not because there is no [interior] truth for us to listen to, just as our eyes do not deceive us for lack of an exterior light by which we should be seeing things. We realize that we must seek that light if we are to behold things according to our physical capacity.

39

Now if we interpret colors by means of light, and other things we sense by the world's physical elements, and the sensations themselves by the soul that uses them as intermediaries, then we must interpret intelligible things by our mind's interior truth—and what could better illustrate the fact that from words in themselves we learn nothing than does the sensation of their sound in our ears? For everything we perceive is perceived either by physical sensation or mental apprehension, giving us either sensible things or intelligible ones—or, as our Christian writers would prefer, objects either carnal or spiritual. If we are questioned about the former, we can answer if the question involves things present to our senses—if, for instance, we are looking at a new moon when asked about its position or phases. If the questioner does not himself see the moon, he has to take my word for it—or, more frequently, refuse to do so. In any case, he does not really learn the facts unless he sees them for himself—in which case, not the sound of the words but the sight of the thing informs his own senses. As far as the words go, they are the same whether one is seeing or not seeing what they describe.

But when we are asked about things not present to our senses now, but perceived by our senses at some prior time, then we are no longer describing things perceived as we speak, but images of them received by our senses in the past and now stored away in our memory. And since we are no longer considering the things themselves, but something they are not, I do not know how we can continue to call our answer a true one unless we admit that we are reporting not what we see or perceive, but what we remember to have seen or perceived. Such images, filed away in the archives of memory, are like documents recording past experiences, and if we scrutinize and report them honestly, we are not lying. Still, they are our own inner documents. If one hearing my report has experienced the same things himself, by his own present sensation, then he learns nothing from my words, but recognizes the same reality he had stored up his own record of. But if he has not experienced the same reality himself, then we must admit that he does not have his own understanding of the thing but a mere trust in my words.

40

If, however, we are dealing with things we perceive in the intellect, using our understanding and reason, then we speak of things perceived directly by the inner light of truth, which enlightens and fertilizes what we have called the interior self. And our listener, if he too perceives them with his own inner and innocent eye, knows what I am describing by his own vision of it, not by my words. In that case, even though I should speak true and he accept it as true, I teach him nothing. He learns not from my words but from the realities themselves, revealed to him by God's action within him. What could be odder than for him to think he was learning from my words what he could have told a questioner before I ever spoke to him?

When, as often happens, a man denies something when first asked about it, and then has to affirm it under harder questioning, this comes from his own weak inner vision, which kept him from submitting the whole matter to truth's inner light. And he is led beyond the part he sees if one asks him about all the parts that make up the matter he had not seen clearly as a whole. And even if words are used to help him on, the words themselves do not teach him, though they afford an occasion for him to consult the inner truth from which he must learn.

If, for instance, I were to ask you (in keeping with our subject) if nothing can be taught by words, the question might seem silly if you were not up to seeing the problem in its entirety. I would be obliged, in that case, to frame my questions in such a way as to direct your talents to what your interior teacher is telling you. And if I were to ask you, "How did you learn to speak the truth when I was questioning you, and to be firm in it, and to say you know that you know it," you might tell me that I was teaching you. But then I would take you a step further, and ask you this: If I told you I saw a man flying, would those words be as convincing to you as if you heard me say that wise men deserve more respect than fools? Naturally, you would say no, telling me you do not believe what I said about flying, and even if you did believe it you would not know it, the way you are certain of the truths you listed. Surely that is enough to make you see that my words taught you nothing—neither when I said I saw a man flying, of which you said you could know nothing, nor when I said about wise men what you knew perfectly well on your own. Indeed, asked about these two points [entirely apart form my words], you would have been prompt to say that the first was unknowable, and the second was readily known.

You would thus have reached the point of admitting on a full view a thing you had denied on a partial view, having put all the elements of the problem together in a clear and certain way to reach this conclusion: Whenever we talk, the one who hears us either does not know whether what we say is true, or does know that it is false, or he knows that it is true. In the first case, he has belief or opinion or doubt; in the second, opposition or denial; in the third, affirmation—and in none of these cases is the hearer being taught. In the first case, he has not grasped a truth from my words, in the second he knows my words are false, and in the third he already knows what I was saying and could have affirmed it without hearing me at all.

41

If this is so, then where inward understanding is at issue, it does no good to hear about another's understanding unless one has the same understanding on one's own—except in cases where *trust* is relied on for the period when one cannot reach understanding. But anyone who is able to reach his own perception is a learner in his internal forum, and a judge of those addressing him in the external forum, or at least a judge of what any person says, since he often understands what is being said though the speaker himself does not. Imagine, for instance, that a man who believes with Epicurus that the soul is mortal should cite sounder persons' arguments in favor of its immortality, and his listener, who has greater spiritual discernment, sees that the words he is citing are true. The speaker, then, who is speaking truths he is unaware of, or rather things he is sure are false—can we say that he is teaching others what he does not know himself? He is, after all, using the same arguments that those who believe in them would use.

42

We can no longer, therefore, claim even this minimal role for words, that at least they express the speaker's views, since he may not realize what he is saying—or in fact he may be lying or misleading others, in which case he is not only failing to express his views, but actually using words to falsify them. I do not deny that some try to express their views in truthful words, even go as it were on oath for their veracity, and they might be believed if we could exclude liars from the process. But we also know from experience that words, our own as well as others', often fail to reflect the speaker's thoughts. I believe two of the ways this can happen are, first, when one recites words familiar to memory and often repeated, while thinking of something entirely different (for instance, while singing a psalm); or, second, by accident, when ill-considered words slip out that misrepresent what one really intended to say, and the signs of things we have in mind are not conveyed to the listener. The opposite of this occurs with the liar, who is extremely conscious of what he is saying. Even if we cannot tell when a liar is telling the truth, we can be sure that he is conveying what he means to—unless one of those two kinds of inadvertence should happen even to him. If one objects that these ways of misleading are uncommon and easily recognized, I have little trouble with that, even though the misdirection often goes unrecognized, and I have often enough been fooled by it.

43

A different category altogether, a common one, the cause of endless wrangling and misunderstanding, involves the person who does express his views, at least for himself and his own coterie, though his words do not have the same meaning for any other who hears them, or for that man's company. Someone might say, for instance, that some animals are brighter than human beings, a proposition we cannot accept, and which we vigorously denounce as false and corrupting—while all the time he just meant that some animals are brighter in color, not in intellect. He was not lying, nor confused in his own mind, nor thinking something different from what he was saying, nor reciting by mindless rote, nor mispeaking by accident. He is merely expressing his thought with a word whose meaning we do not share with him. We would agree with him at once if we could read his mind, which remains closed to us, though he has spoken accurately about what he is thinking.

Some say this problem can be solved by careful definition—in this case, for instance, by defining what one means by brightness. They say that will make it clear that one is wrangling over words, not things. Even if I should accept that, there are few men who can make accurate definitions. And there are, besides, theoretical difficulties about the act of defining, which this is not the time for us to entertain, even if I knew (and I don't) how to resolve them.

44

Another problem I pass by is the frequency with which we conduct energetic disputes over words imperfectly heard, though we think we heard them clearly. Not long ago I told you a certain word means "mercy" in Punic, but you said you had heard from those better acquainted with the language that it means "piety." I doubted that, and said you must have forgotten what you were given as the meaning, since I had heard what you said as "faith"—even though you were close to me as you spoke, and the words do not sound at all alike. For some time I thought you did not know what you were saying, when it was really I who did not know what you were saying. If I had heard you properly, it would not have seemed odd for the Punic language to use the same word for both mercy and faith. This is not an isolated occurrence, but I shall, as I said, pass it by, lest I seem to be convicting words themselves of their users' carelessness or mere defect of hearing. But the cases I mentioned earlier are more troublesome, where we cannot understand what the speaker has in mind, even though he voices it with perfect diction and in the Latin language we share with him.

45

But even if I stipulate that it is possible, when we recognize words being spoken, that a speaker's views can be ascertained from those words, does that mean that we ascertain the *truth* of those views, which is what we are concerned with? Do teachers advertise that they verbally transmit their own acts of understanding, or the truths of their discipline, for students to receive and retain? What father sends a child to school with the silly aim of finding out what the teacher's understanding is? Rather, when all subjects, even those concerning virtue and wisdom, have been expounded by those who profess them, then students, if they are really to be called that, investigate within themselves whether what they are hearing is true, strenuously putting it to the test of their own interior truth. That is the point at which they learn. And when they reach an inner conviction of truth, they praise their teachers, not realizing that, even if the teachers knew what they were saying, the praise rightly belongs to the taught ones not the ones who taught. Men make the mistake of calling others their teachers when they are no such thing, since there is a near-simultaneity between what is said and what is understood, and where inner assent follows so quickly on outer discussion they think the latter caused the former.

46

We may, God willing, get around later on to a general consideration of the use of words—properly undertaken, that is a major project. My only caution for now is that you not ascribe to them greater power than belongs to them. We should resolve to bring reasoned understanding, not mere pious acceptance, to the text given us by divine authority, that we should call no man our teacher, since 'the single teacher of all men is he who dwells in heaven' [Matthew 23.10]. The meaning of the words 'in heaven' he will himself teach us, who provides us the external occasion, through others' words, to submit to his internal schooling. Knowing and loving him make up the blessed life, which all say they want to attain, though few can feel assured that they have found it.

Tell me, finally, what you made of this whole speech to

you. If you found any truth in what I said, you can assure anyone who asks that you already knew it, down to the finest points—which shows that you realize who was really teaching you. It was not I, though you were responding to things I said. But if you found no truth at all in my words, then no one taught you—not he, and not I. Not I, because there is nothing that I can teach. And not he, because there was nothing that you learned.

S By the occasion your words provided, I have learned that words can do no more than provide such an occasion for learning; that words cannot even tell us much about the thoughts of those using them; and that their truth is to be established only by our internal teacher, who provides external words only as an occasion for me to love him more ardently, with his help, and learn in proportion as I love.

As for your speech, it *was* a long one, though I am glad of that, since you anticipated and removed objections I was ready to make, leaving out no point I would have raised, and each thing I learned from my own internal oracle corresponded with your words.

Notes

1. Windings of the tune: *modulationem quandam*. In *Music* 5, Augustine says that *modulare* means to arrange the intervals in pitch and tempo.
2. Augustine artfully chooses a line, from his vast repertoire of remembered Virgilian verses, that begins with three tricky words—*Si nihil ex*—just the kind Wittgenstein said Augustine overlooked in his theory of language (see *comm.* [13]). Godsend has to take them

in order. The translation cannot keep these words at the head of the verse, unless I resort to some periphrasis that would involve more words than eight. So Godsend takes the words out of order in the translation.

3. Since Godsend is about to say that *audibilia* is an odd form ("hearable"), its parallel *visibilia* should be formed to match it.

4. Deaf "signing" and military standards are Augustine's regular examples of nonverbal symbol systems—see *Christian Culture* 2.3.4, cited in *comm.* **[8]**. For the importance of sign language to the study of modern linguistics, see Noam Chomsky, *The Architecture of Language* (Oxford University Press, 2000), pp. 9, 50–52, 66.

5. The etymologies are as forced in the Latin, and more like puns than serious arguments, an important clue to the "jousting" nature of this part of the dialogue, its "limbering up" part. "Whir" is *verberare*, "impinge"—since Augustine thought hearing resulted from a stir in the fine air of the ear, which the soul went out to "seize." The *noun-know* pun *(nomen-nosco)* is not equally absurd; it has some linguistic basis.

6. Augustine's Latin Bible misrepresented the original Greek, which said "yes and no" where he read "is and is not."

7. Augustine, with his view of conversation with others as a stimulant to the internal teacher, says that one often learns by teaching others—see *Christian Culture*, Preface 12 and *comm.* **[13]**.

8. Compare *Music* 6.1.

9. Augustine asks whether "man is man," but the later breaking of the word into syllables makes it impossible to use a monosyllable in the translation, or an equivalent like "human" since one of its syllables, *man*, is a word in itself. Masculine is the closest I could come in English. *Mas* is *male* in Latin, but I am using the *English* word in the translation.

10. The pun *ordure-order* is, in Latin, *coenum-coelum* (excrement-heaven).

11. "Afford an occasion" is the meaning Burnyeat finds in *admonere*.